THE NEW RED LION INN COOKBOOK

THE NEW RED LION INN COOKBOOK

Suzi Forbes Chase

BERKSHIRE HOUSE PUBLISHERS
Lee, Massachusetts

We gratefully acknowledge permission from the following publishers to use excerpts from the following authors:

American Cookery, by James Beard, copyright © 1972, Little, Brown and Company; *The American Heritage Cookbook,* by The Editors of *American Heritage, the Magazine of History,* copyright © 1964, 1969; *General Foods Cookbook,* by The Women of General Foods Kitchen, copyright © 1959, Random House; *New England Cookbook,* Eleanor Early, copyright © 1954, Random House, Inc.

Color photography by A. Blake Gardner

THE RED LION INN COOKBOOK

Edited by Constance L. Oxley
Cover, book design, and typesetting by Jane McWhorter, Blue Sky Productions
Index by Elizabeth T. Parson

Library of Congress Cataloging in Publication Data

Chase, Suzi Forbes.
The new Red Lion Inn cookbook / Suzi Forbes Chase.—Rev. ed.
p. cm.
Includes bibliographical references and index.
ISBN 158157-012-0
1. Cookery, American—New England style. 2. Red Lion Inn (Stockbridge, Mass.) I. Title.

TX715.2.N48.C44 2000
641.5974—dc21   99-087036

ISBN 1-58157-012-0
Printed in Singapore
First printing 2000
10 9 8 7 6 5 4 3 2 1

To my beloved mother, Margaret Sutton, who inspired me to appreciate and cook a variety of cuisines, and who passed away in 1999, and to my grandmother, Minnie Kerner, who patiently taught me all her culinary secrets.

Acknowledgments

The first edition of The Red Lion Inn Cookbook was written in 1992, and it reflected the traditional cuisine that has characterized the Red Lion Inn through most of its 200+ years. Under the leadership of Nancy Fitzpatrick, who began overseeing the operations in 1992, the Red Lion Inn has emerged as one of the premiere dining rooms of Berkshire County, and it has developed such a fine wine list that it recently won a Wine Spectator Award. Therefore, although many of the time-honored and most-loved recipes have been retained, this new cookbook also reflects the cutting edge new cuisine that characterizes the restaurants today.

Writing a cookbook is never an individual accomplishment, but an orchestrated collaboration involving chefs, executive staff, photographers, and publishing house personnel. Therefore, I have numerous individuals that I would like to acknowledge.

Executive Chef Douglas Luf, a graduate of the Culinary Institute of America, has been redefining The Red Lion Inn's cuisine ever since his arrival in the mid-1990s. His expertise and inventive culinary ideas have created a distinctive Contemporary New American cuisine. I owe him a tremendous measure of thanks for his patience in reducing his recipe quantities from inn-size to home-size and for tolerantly answering my many questions as I developed the recipe instructions and tested the recipes. In addition, his artist's eye for food composition was an invaluable aid during the photography phase of the book.

Chris Pavao, the Director of Food and Beverage for The Red Lion Inn, was the point person for this project. Decisions about new and old recipes, coordination with Brooks Bradbury, the Red Lion Innkeeper, Nancy Fitzpatrick, Chef Luf, and myself, photography scheduling and layouts, as well as a myriad of questions were filtered through his capable hands. He handled them all with composure, equanimity, and aplomb. Jayne Church, Manager of the Pink Kitty Gift Shop, Alta Stark, Marketing Manager, Cindy Kelly and Isabelle Soule, Nancy Fitzpatrick's assistants, were invaluable in their quest for wonderful props to use during the photo shoot.

The photographer, A. Blake Gardner, has considerable experience in food and travel photography. His unflappable composure, his boundless energy, and his artistic eye all collaborated to create the fine photographs you see on these pages.

I would also like to thank Jean Rousseau and Philip Rich, Publisher and Editor of Berkshire House Publishers respectively, for their professionalism, support, and friendship. My editor for this book, Constance L. Oxley, was my editor on a previous book as well, and I feel very fortunate. She brought sound common sense to the project coupled with genuine enthusiasm for the subject. She took an interest that extended far beyond that of most editors - and even tested several recipes herself when she was unsure about quantities or instructions. Carol Bosco Baumann, Marketing Director for Berkshire House, is one of the finest publicists I have ever worked with. She is enthusiastic, tremendously hardworking and imaginative. If she can't place a story, I don't see how anyone can. I would also like to thank Berkshire House office manager, Mary Osak, who is always cheerful on the telephone and keeps all the paper-work straight.

Finally, thanks go to my husband, Dustin Chase, who has enjoyed many wonderful meals with me at The Red Lion Inn, especially when we lived in Stockbridge. We've spent treasured Thanksgiving and Christmas dinners here, as well as birthday celebrations and even a black tie ball on New Years Eve. So for us, as well as for many of you, my fondest hope is that we will all be able to recreate many of our most cherished memories through the use of this cookbook — and may it inspire you to return many times in the future to this gracious and venerable country inn.

Contents

The New Red Lion Inn Cookbook

CHAPTER 1

The History of The Red Lion Inn

Although the *Mayflower* landed at Plymouth in the Massachusetts Bay Colony in 1620, it was another century before Stockbridge in western Massachusetts was settled. In 1736, John Sergeant, the first missionary to the Mahican Indians . . . a branch of the Algonquins, established a crude settlement at a horseshoe bend in the serpentine Housatonic River. By 1737, the tiny village was considered permanent enough for incorporation, adopting the name of Stockbridge, after the town of the same name in Hampshire County, England.

Stockbridge was on the post road from Albany to Boston. As horseback travel increased, so did the necessity to feed and house weary travelers. Thus, taverns were established along its length. Eventually, the crude trails were widened to accommodate stagecoaches, and tavern business steadily increased.

Norman Simpson, a Berkshire County resident and author, explained the prolif-

eration of these taverns in a 1971 article in the *Boston Globe*. "In Puritan Massachusetts, 'ordinaries' (taverns) were established as quickly as churches in new communities. A 1656 proclamation by the General Court fined towns without public houses. . . . Taverns, in which news from the outside world was daily posted and discussed, were truer town centers than the church or village green."

Allan Forbes and Ralph M. Eastman describe the typical tavern in their delightful book *Taverns and Stagecoaches of New England*. "Coaches usually traveled at the rate of four or five miles an hour with a change of horses every ten miles. This gave passengers the opportunity to refresh themselves at the taverns along the way. It was customary for the stage to arrive at an inn at the hour of noon when a hearty dinner, the chief meal of the day, was ready for the travelers. When it came to overnight lodging, there was no such thing as a private room.

The famous Red Lion Inn logo with web site added.

All beds were big enough to accommodate at least two persons, and frequently there were as many as three beds in a room. The tavern keeper did not consider his house filled until every bed was yielding at least double income. If a guest wanted a bath or a fire in the room, there was an extra charge.

The fire was kindled to order in the fire-place, or stove, and the bath was taken in a wooden tub, which a porter filled with hot water carried up from the kitchen."

The busy Albany-Boston turnpike spawned many taverns and stagecoach stops, and The Red Lion Inn was one of the most popular. Most historians place its birth at 1773, although considerable scholarly research by Lion G. Miles, a freelance historical researcher specializing in eigh-teenth-century America, indicates The Red Lion Inn may have been established as late as 1778 (See "Anna Bingham: From The Red Lion Inn to the Supreme Court" in *The New England Quarterly*). It's possible, due to the paucity of written property transfer records, other historians may have confused the existence of a tavern that actually ex-

Main Street, Stockbridge, turn of the century. The old Red Lion Inn, or Stockbridge House, is on the left.

A view of the porch of The Red Lion Inn, 1894

isted across the street with the history of The Red Lion Inn.

Mr. Miles says that Silas and Anna Bingham started a country store on the prominent north-south road through Berkshire County sometime in 1775. It appears that about 1778, they expanded their store and offered overnight accommodations, as well as food and drink. In 1781, Silas died, but plucky Anna continued to operate her inn until sometime between 1796 and 1800, at which time she no longer used her home as a tavern.

When the prominent jurist Theodore Sedgwick moved to Stockbridge with his family in 1785, there was limited stagecoach travel, although horseback journeys and those by private carriages were common. His daughter Catherine Sedgwick, destined to become an acclaimed American author, wrote that "there were no steamers, no railroads, and a stage route through our valley but once a week. Gentlemen made their journeys in private carriages. Yet, insidiously, the outer world was creeping in."

Stagecoach travel steadily increased to three times a week by 1807, then to once a day, and eventually to eight times a day — four in each direction, stopping for a rest and change of horses at the Stockbridge Tavern.

In 1807, Widow Bingham sold her inn to Silas Pepoon, and in 1812 he sold it to Jonathan Hicks (or it may have been transferred to Hicks as part of Pepoon's bancruptcy proceedings, according to Mr. Miles).

For the next forty years, the tavern's fortunes were meager. To a proper English family that moved to Stockbridge in the 1820s, temporarily staying at J. Hicks's Inn, it seemed uncivilized, coarse, and almost barbaric. The daughter, Anne Ashburner, wrote that "the red-faced owner, Mr. Hicks, and his fat, good-natured wife seemed the essence of vulgarity and just the persons to keep such an inn."

With the Sedgwicks in town, however, the social and intellectual scene buzzed. In 1835, the famous English actress Fanny Kemble came to Stockbridge to visit with Catherine Sedgwick, eventually making nearby Lenox her home, despite her claim that there was no good bread in all of

Berkshire County. (She sent Catherine a recipe for "effervescing bread" to overcome this flaw.)

And then the railroad came. As early as 1826 Theodore Sedgwick had proposed a railroad through Stockbridge, but progress was slow. In 1838, however, the Hudson-Berkshire Railroad completed a three-mile spur from Stateline, New York, to West Stockbridge (about five miles from Stockbridge), so for twelve years passengers bound for The Red Lion Inn arrived at the tiny depot in West Stockbridge and traveled the rest of the way by stagecoach. Finally, in 1850, the Berkshire branch of the New Haven & Hartford Railroad from New York was completed, depositing throngs of people at the Stockbridge station every summer. Eventually two express trains made the trip daily in four hours.

In 1848, the *Pittsfield Sun* described the inn, now named the Stockbridge House again: "[It] contains four pleasant and airy Parlours, a spacious Dining Hall, and thirty-four large and well-ventilated rooms. Bathing Rooms are attached to the House . . . A superior Livery Stable is attached to the House and horses and carriages will be ready at a moments notice and for a moderate charge."

In the mid-nineteenth century, numerous literary icons visited The Red Lion Inn. William Cullen Bryant, who was born in Berkshire County and practiced law in Great Barrington, returned to the Berkshires frequently after he moved to New York. In 1850, Nathanial Hawthorne came to nearby Lenox looking "for a cheap, pleasant, and healthy residence." Hawthorne had just written *The Scarlet Letter* and was offered a small red house at the north end of the Stockbridge Bowl, in a location that must have seemed extremely remote at the time. Nevertheless, Herman Melville, who owned a house some eight miles distant in Pittsfield, walked over to visit Hawthorne often. It was here that Hawthorne wrote *The House of the Seven Gables*, among other tales.

Oliver Wendell Holmes and Henry Wadsworth Longfellow came, too, both occupying homes in Pittsfield, and probably taking many meals at The Red Lion Inn. In 1853, Henry Ward Beecher owned a nearby house, where he spent several summers.

In the two-hundred-plus-year history of The Red Lion Inn, fortune seems to have brought saviors to its door just when the inn's future seemed least promising. In 1862, the inn was purchased by Mr. and Mrs. Charles H. Plumb, beginning a family tenure that extended three generations. A remarkable ninety-year span from the Plumbs, to their nephew Allen T. Treadway, to his son Heaton I. Treadway — brought stability and prosperity to the inn. Charles and "Aunt Mert," as she was called, lavished attention and love on the old inn.

Aunt Mert knew antiques, and with a practiced eye she roamed the countryside, rescuing treasures for the Stockbridge House parlors, bedrooms, and dining rooms. Reputedly, the first antique purchased for the inn was the magnificent grandfather clock that stands today beside the elevator. It is dated 1790 and, as the story goes, was purchased for $10. Another notable antique is the large mahogany table that once served as the dining room table in New York's Union League Club. It is said to have been dined upon by Thackeray, Lincoln, and Dickens, among others. It now holds a place of prominence in the center of the lobby.

With a droll sense of humor, Heaton Treadway described many of the antiques in *The Tale of the Lion* — witty tales told by the Red Lion himself (whether they are truth or pure fiction, we'll never know). They were published originally on the back of the Sunday menus and later printed in a pamphlet. The tales contain whimsical accounts of Aunt Mert's discoveries, such as the following: "Some of us speculate in stocks, some of us in Florida real estate, and I limit mine to buying and collecting secondhand furniture, and I haven't done too badly. The sideboard in the back of the dining room is a remarkable piece in that it has the original maker's label on each of the cabinet doors. It was found by 'Aunt Mert' being used as a chicken coop. She paid $3.50 for this piece of secondhand junk. It is a piece of Hepplewhite and was made by William Whitehead, Cabinet and Chair

Maker, Pearl Street, New York City. It is his card that is pasted on the inside of the cabinet doors." The sideboard continues to grace the inn today.

Word spread quickly through the countryside that "Aunt Mert" would pay "fifty cents for any teapot and a dollar for any mirror." Many of the teapots that line shelves in the parlors and the mirrors in the hallways and bedrooms were brought to The Red Lion Inn from neighboring farms and houses. Then as now, however, the

A view of Mrs. Plumb's private parlor, 1894, in the inn then known as the Stockbridge House.

STOCKBRIDGE LIBRARY ASSOCIATION HISTORICAL ROOM

splendid antique collection adorns the inn for the enjoyment of the guests. Mr. Treadway once said, "You must remember that the inn is the home of the guest. In his own home, he admires his antiques and other objects of art at his own leisure. It is our desire that he enjoy the same freedom and pleasure at the inn."

In 1884, the Plumbs increased the inn's size to accommodate up to one hundred guests. They equipped each room with a

On August 31, 1896, a fire devastated The Red Lion Inn (then known as the Stockbridge House).

THE RED LION INN

Franklin stove or fireplace, which was lighted every evening to ward off the chill. In 1893, they added yet another wing and a new dining room. And then disaster struck.

On August 31, 1896, a fire started in the pastry kitchen and soon spread throughout the inn. Flames engulfed room after room, until only a black skeleton of Stockbridge House remained. Fortunately, there were no injuries and townsfolk formed a brigade to save the collections of furniture, paintings, Colonial china, teapots, mirrors, and clothes.

Undaunted, the Plumbs and Treadways immediately rebuilt the inn and a mere eight months later an elegant new building rose from the ashes. Christened The Red

Lion Inn, it was larger, grander, and safer than the old version, although it retained the Colonial charm of the original. Praise and acclaim attended the opening of the new inn. It was noted that brick fire-stops had been placed between partitions to prevent a similar conflagration in the future. A thoughtful addition to the new inn was the special "women's door" that led to a women's reception room and parlor — a place where the ladies could rest after their journey, while their bags were being fetched and their rooms prepared. A women's retiring room at the far end of the entrance hall was used by women who had journeyed to the inn for the day only.

A chapter in *Taverns and Stagecoaches of*

New England describes the rebuilt Red Lion Inn: "When the present building was constructed, it was in a period when it was considered unsanitary to sleep in a room adjoining a toilet. Because of this, only two private bathrooms were provided in the whole establishment. It was customary then for seasonal guests to bring their own bathtubs, and it was nothing out of the ordinary after the arrival of the evening train to have to deliver twenty or twenty-five bathtubs an evening to the rooms, along with trunks and other luggage. The natural sequence was not too much appreciated by the maids of the inn as they had to take on the onerous duty of carrying hot water to the various rooms that harbored the traveling bathtubs."

The new inn boasted larger dining rooms, grander parlors and reception rooms, a total of twenty-two fireplaces, and eighty guest rooms. The grand "piazza" (we call it the front porch today) extended the length of the inn, right on Main Street, and was placed high enough above street level that Joseph Choate, a prominent New York lawyer, who summered in Stockbridge, was led to remark, "If anyone sat long enough on the Red Lion "piazza," he would see pass everybody worth knowing." That would have included President William McKinley, who came to Stockbridge shortly after the new inn opened to wish Choate well in his new position as U.S. Ambassador to Great Britain.

Even this new modern inn, however, was not equipped with central heating (nor were the elaborate summer "cottages" built by wealthy New Yorkers in the surrounding hills). The inn would open each April and close sometime in November. Rachel Field, an author from a prominent Stockbridge family, remarked, "It was winter not so much when the first snow fell as when The Red Lion Inn put up its shutters, after the departure of the last city visitor." An attempt to open the inn year-round as recently as 1960 failed, and the famous 1967 painting by Stockbridge resident Norman Rockwell called *Stockbridge at Christmas* includes a dark, shuttered Red Lion Inn hibernating through the winter months.

Touring cars were the mode of transportation to the inn by the early 1900s, and a stately procession of elegant automobiles could be seen parked in front of the grand "piazza." In 1935, Mrs. Calvin (Grace) Coolidge, wife of the former president, was the first to sign the guest book for the summer season. A humorous story is told about Calvin Coolidge. It seems that he once visited the inn on his way to Great Bar-

> "All that is left of it is a portion of the front part, which is of no use, and will simply have to be torn down. The hotel was insured for $20,000, and the contents for $5,000. The loss is estimated at fully $50,000. It was the most disastrous fire that ever visited the town. The fire was discovered at 4:30 a.m. by the night watchman. He discovered flames bursting forth from the pastry kitchen in the rear of the house."
>
> — *The Berkshire Evening Eagle*, "Stockbridge Inn Gone" August 31, 1896

"It takes a heap of living in an Inn to make it right,
A heap of sun and shadow, both the sad days and the bright.
It takes a lot of caring for the welfare of the guests
To know, before they ask you, how to answer their requests.
It's not the chairs and tables nor the shingles on the roof,
But the wanting others happy that furnishes the proof.

A real Inn can't be bought, or built, or made up in a minute,
To make an Inn there's got to be a heap of living in it.
The singing and the laughter have to work into the wood,
And stoves get used to cooking so that meals are downright good.
The staff must fit together as a smoothly working whole
Through the long cooperation there of every single soul.

You need good beds and linens, and a lovely village too,
But the things that really matter are the old things, not the new; —
The age-old smile of welcome and the well-worn wish to please,
The years of long experience that put a guest at ease,
The gracious hospitality for travelers who roam,
And the long familiarity that makes folk feel at home.

The Treadways up in Stockbridge, at the old Red Lion sign,
Have an Inn that they've been running now for season eighty-nine.
Old friends will know that here's a place to spend a grand vacation,
New England hospitality is the best in all the nation.
Near symphony at Tanglewood, near Stockbridge Players too,
Not far from Ted Shawn's Dancers, all waiting here for you;
With the Berkshire Hills around you, far from urban heat and din,
Come and join us up in Stockbridge at the famed Red Lion Inn.

The Fitzpatricks have been running it, the old Red Lion Inn,
Its years are now two hundred; we hope you will come in.
Near skiing down at Butternut, near Norman Rockwell's paintings, too,
Not far from Bousquet skiing, all waiting here for you.
With the Berkshire Hills around you, far from urban crowd and din,
Come and join us up in Stockbridge at the famed Red Lion Inn."

— The Reverend Alfred B. Starrett, former rector of St. Paul's Episcopal Church, directly across Main Street from The Red Lion Inn, penned this poem in 1951. He added the final stanza in 1973 to celebrate the inn's bicentennial.

rooms so that almost all rooms now have private baths. A former lounge was turned into the Widow Bingham's Tavern, a modern kitchen was installed, and the inn today enjoys the amenities of a modern hotel within a historic structure. In 1983, the quaint, Victorian iron-lace elevator in the lobby was restored, and it was converted from a water to an oil hydraulic system, allowing it to remain in use year-round.

Not only have the Fitzpatricks thoroughly restored and renovated the rooms in the main inn, they have purchased many of the charming houses surrounding the inn and converted them to guest rooms and suites. The Stafford House, O'Brien House, Stevens House, Maple House, McGregor House, and The Old Fire House, all contain elegant and/or whimsical accommodations. The Old Fire House, the wonderful white clapboard building with red trim that was Stockbridge's first fire station, contains a charming and debonair suite that is much sought after by those in the know.

Today, formal dining is in the Main Dining Room, which is lined with fine paintings and filled with antiques. Informal dining takes place in the Widow Bingham's Tavern or downstairs in the Lion's Den, which also offers nighttime entertainment. In the summer, the Courtyard, which is filled with planters of bright impatiens and umbrella-topped tables under spreading elm trees, offers cool outdoor dining.

A spacious Country Curtains shop provides guests with a myriad of ideas about window treatments, as well as an array of gift selections, while the Pink Kitty Gift Shop supplements the gift supply with greeting cards, books, games, and elegant treasures. In 1993, following the tradition established by the Plumb/Treadway families, Jack and Jane Fitzpatrick's daughter, Nancy, began supervising the inn. Her commitment to exceptional cuisine is winning high praise for The Red Lion Inn's dining room, and the expanded wine cellar has garnered an award from *The Wine Spectator*.

Great patrons of the arts, Jack and Jane Fitzpatrick have been driving forces behind the Boston Symphony Orchestra and its summer home at Tanglewood in nearby Lenox, as well as the Berkshire Theatre Festival and the Norman Rockwell Museum. In 1998, the Berkshire Theatre Festival celebrated its seventieth anniversary. The gala program, which included a concert by James Taylor and a sketch of the couple by Al Hirschfeld, was dedicated to the Fitzpatricks in thanks for their more than twenty years of support. Also in 1998, the Fitzpatrick family were the recipients of the Paul E. Tsongas Award from Historic Massachusetts in recognition of their exceptional role in preserving the historic and cultural heritage of the Commonwealth.

Famous guests continue to make the pilgrimage to The Red Lion Inn. John Wayne stayed at the inn in 1973, while Norman Rockwell painted his portrait for the National Cowboy Hall of Fame in Oklahoma City. He became a familiar sight in below-freezing weather, striding across the porch in a cowboy hat and a Western-cut role in the creation of the United States. The American Revolution was, after all, a rebellion based on taxes levied against New Englander's pocketbooks and on their food — on such items as tea, molasses, and Madeira. John Adams once said, in reference to the Molasses Act passed by the British Parliament in 1733, "I know not why we should blush to confess that molasses is an essential ingredient in American independence."

The seeds that were brought by the early settlers for common English crops proved difficult to grow, but the Pilgrims had fled from a government that they distrusted, so they refused to seek help from England, even when threatened with starvation. Instead, they adapted their knowledge of food preparation to indigenous crops: corn, beans, and squash. It was that or live only on fish. This forced them to build a self-sustaining agricultural system in just one generation.

They learned to dry and pulverize corn, for example, and when they did, they found that they could separate the finest granules to form a corn flour. It stubbornly created coarse and crumbly breads, however, which refused to rise as did breads made with wheat and rye flours. So the Pilgrim women made a thin batter with corn flour and water and poured it on a griddle. And that's how johnnycake, a delectable pancake loved by New Englanders, was born.

Benjamin Franklin was especially fond of johnnycakes. In 1766, he wrote in the *Gazetteer,* in reply to an Englishman who had said Indian corn was not "an agreeable ...breakfast": "Pray, let me, an American, inform the gentleman, who seems ignorant of the matter, that Indian corn, take it for all in all, is one of the most agreeable and wholesome grains in the world. . . and that johnny or hoecake, hot from the fire, is better than a Yorkshire muffin."

The Pilgrims learned that if they boiled the corn with water, they had a nice mush for a hot breakfast treat, or to serve with meat at dinner. Roger Williams described hasty pudding in 1643 in *A Key into the Language of America* as "a kind of meale pottage, unpartch'd. From this the English call their Samp, which is the Indian corne, beaten, and boiled, and eaten hot or cold with milk or butter. . . and which is a dish exceeding wholesome for the English

---

John Ruskin (1819-1900), an English essayist, critic, and reformer, wrote about being a lady: "Cookery means the knowledge of Medea and of Circe and of Helen and of the Queen of Sheba. It means the knowledge of all herbs and fruits and balms and spices, and all that is healing and sweet in the fields and groves and savory in meats. It means carefulness and inventiveness and willingness and readiness of appliances. It means the economy of your grandmothers and the science of the modern chemist; it means much testing and no wasting; it means English thoroughness and French art and Arabian hospitality; and, in fine, it means that you are to be perfectly and always, ladies — loaf givers."

The lone car parked in front of The Red Lion Inn seems to place this postcard in the 1940s.

bodies." Leftover corn mush (never let it be said a New England housewife wasted anything!) was formed into blocks, sliced, fried, and eaten with maple syrup or molasses.

Indian pudding, a concoction of cornmeal, milk, eggs, sugar, butter, and cinnamon, was another popular treat. The Red Lion Inn recipe for Indian pudding is a very old one that has been served at the inn for well over a hundred years. Indian pudding, however, was not a dish the Indians invented. Rather, the name was devised to distinguish the yellow Indian kernel used in the pudding from English corn, which we know as wheat. Thus, a dish made from Indian corn was called Indian pudding.

Beans were also of utmost importance to the Pilgrims, partly because they were plentiful, which made them cheap, and partly because they were so integral to the observation of the Sabbath. No work was allowed on the Sabbath, which extended from sundown Saturday to sundown Sunday — not even cooking. So the pot of beans went into the brick oven on Friday night and emerged, in the form of piping-hot baked beans, in time for the Saturday night meal. Traditionally, this hearty feast was served with a brown bread. The saying went "Brown bread and the Gospel is good fare." Baked beans were eaten for breakfast on Sunday and again when the family returned from church on Sunday afternoon. Every week this ritual was repeated. Later, baked beans became popular tavern fare. The Red Lion Inn's version is based on the earliest traditional recipes.

If Saturday was baked beans and brown bread day, Wednesday in New England was boiled dinner day, just as surely as Thursday was reserved for corned beef hash, using the leftovers from Wednesday's meal. Friday was fish day — sometimes a hearty chowder, such as the version found in Chapter 4.

"Fath'r and I went down to camp
Along with Captain Goodin,
And there we saw the men and boys
As thick as hasty puddin'."

— Yankee Doodle,
Eighteenth-century song

dinners are provided, consisting of almost everything in season. The hour is from two to three o'clock, and there are three meals in the day. They breakfast at eight o'clock upon rump steaks, fish, eggs, and a variety of cakes with tea or coffee. The last meal is at seven in the evening and consists of as substantial fare as the breakfast, with the addition of cold fowl, ham, etc. . . . Brandy, hollands, and other spirits are allowed at dinner, but every other liquor is paid for extra. English breakfasts and teas, generally speaking, are meager repasts compared with those of America, and as far as I observed the people live with respect to eating in a much more luxurious manner than we do."

Stockbridge was charmingly described by another member of Stockbridge's Sedgwick family, Henry Dwight; he and his many cousins spent every summer at the family homestead. He relates: "The store [probably across the street from The Red Lion Inn] was a place to linger in, stare at cans, at bags of merchandise, ploughs, bridles, rope, candies under the glass case, all of which told stories of the wide and varied lands from which they came; and there you met your acquaintances, Mike Farley, a big, broad-shouldered, burly, smiling, jolly good fellow, and such. You bought dried hams at the store, but for fresh meat you welcomed Roger Barry, who came everyday with his sorrel nag and his covered wagon."

The food served today at The Red Lion Inn is a reflection of New England's historic heritage. The stockpot is always brewing! The chef explains: "The Red Lion Inn menu is the billboard of traditional New England fare, but of the 1990s and beyond — not two hundred years ago. We've adapted traditional New England recipes for today's healthy attitudes." And now, we welcome you to do the same.

President Coolidge, who visited The Red Lion Inn before and after becoming president, was once asked what was his greatest disappointment in the White House. He replied in typical New England fashion, and without the slightest hesitation, that it was his inability to find out what happened with the leftovers.

— The First Ladies Cook Book, 1966

CHAPTER 3

Appetizers & Hors d'Oeuvres

Generally, hors d'oeuvres and canapés are the finger foods that are served at a cocktail party or a stand-up gathering before a dinner, and appetizers are the light, first courses served at sit-down dinners — but, of course, many dishes can be used both ways.

Irma S. Rombauer and Marion Rombauer Becker, in their wonderful encyclopedia of food preparation, *Joy of Cooking,* describe the difference between hors d'oeuvres and canapés, as well as the pros and cons of eating both before dinner. "Hors d'oeuvres and canapés are appetizers served with drinks. The canapé sits on its own little couch of crouton or pastry tidbit, while the hors d'oeuvre is independent and ready to meet up with whatever bread or cracker is presented separately. Many hors d'oeuvres are themselves rich in fat or are combined with an oil or butter base to buffer the impact of alcohol on the system. If, during preprandial drinking, the appetizer intake is too extensive, any true enjoyment of the meal itself is destroyed. The palate is too heavily coated, too overstimulated by spices and dulled by alcohol."

First-course appetizers have been popular starters for dinner parties for many years. Indeed, before Prohibition in 1920, entertaining was often on a lavish scale. Many-coursed dinner parties were served by legions of servants. There might be three or four appetizers presented before the entrée. Some of the Berkshire dinner parties, which were hosted by Vanderbilts, Westinghouses, Stokeses, Fosters, and Sloanes, were said to be so elaborate that there were up to ten courses and two or three servants were sometimes assigned to each guest.

During the Depression, most Americans didn't have the time or the money to enter-

tain on such a lavish scale. So, after Prohibition was over in 1933, the cocktail party
was devised. It was a relatively inexpensive
way to entertain a large gathering of friends.

Cocktail parties remain a popular way
of entertaining today. The Red Lion Inn is
noted for the parties that it caters, from
large corporate Christmas festivities, to
small private dinner parties, to both inti-
mate and elaborate wedding receptions. A
popular summer cocktail food at The Red
Lion Inn is a huge silver bowl filled with
juicy fresh strawberries, served with con-

fectioners' sugar. Another popular offering
is a large bowl of fresh shrimp with a tangy
cocktail sauce.

Every afternoon The Red Lion Inn staff
sets out a tray of cheese and crackers for
the enjoyment of their guests. In the winter, guests enjoy sitting in the lobby, where
a blazing fire takes the chill off cold noses.
In the summer, the preferred spot is the
spacious porch, which is filled with comfortable wicker rocking chairs and arm-
chairs dressed with pretty chintz cushions.

"Our life is nothing but a winter's day;
Some only breakfast and away;
Others to dinner stay and are full fed.
The deepest age but sups and goes to bed.
He's worst in debt who lingers out the day.
Who goes betimes has all the less to pay."

— Old Tavern Song

Smoked Salmon Red Lion

8 ounces thinly sliced smoked salmon (about 8 slices)
1 cup sour cream
8 teaspoons prepared coarse mustard
4 teaspoons finely chopped fresh dill
4 very thin slices red onion
4 teaspoons capers
thinly sliced pumpernickel bread

1. Arrange the slices of smoked salmon on a serving plate.
2. Thoroughly mix the sour cream, mustard, and dill in a small bowl and spoon over the salmon.
3. Garnish with the onion slices and capers.
4. Serve with the pumpernickel bread in a basket alongside.

SERVES 4

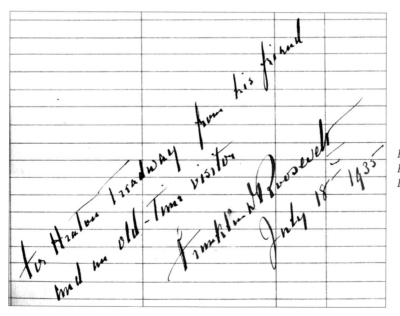

President Franklin Delano Roosevelt's signature in The Red Lion Inn's guest book.

Scallops & Bacon Dijon

When using bacon to wrap scallops or any other food, it is important to partially cook the bacon first to eliminate some of the fat and water before broiling or roasting. This bite-sized hors d'oeuvre is often top on the list of requests at The Red Lion Inn cocktail parties.

20 fresh sea scallops
2 tablespoons white wine
2 tablespoons Dijon mustard
$1/_8$ teaspoon salt
pinch black pepper
10 strips uncooked bacon
20 wooden toothpicks

1. Wash and clean the scallops. Pat dry.
2. Combine the wine, mustard, salt, and black pepper in a bowl and mix together well. Add the scallops and toss to coat. Marinate, covered, in the refrigerator for 1 hour.
3. Preheat oven to 250° F. Arrange the bacon slices in a single layer on a baking sheet and cook in the oven until soft, about 10 minutes. Drain on paper towels. Cut each slice in half crosswise. Increase oven temperature to 350°.
4. Drain the scallops. Wrap a bacon strip around each scallop and fasten it with a toothpick.
5. Arrange the scallops on a baking sheet and bake for 8-10 minutes, basting once with the liquid. Serve hot.

SERVES 10

Escargots Red Lion Inn with Escargot Butter

According to the *Joy of Cooking*, the Romans loved snails so much that they grew them on ranches and fed them a diet of bay leaf, wine, and spicy soups. M.F.K. Fisher, in *The Art of Eating*, describes a visit to the French countryside outside Dijon, where she and her friends gathered a prodigious number of snails from the woods and fields. She said that the French eat about fifty million snails a year. American's love of escargots is not that addictive, but the dish has remained a popular appetizer in top restaurants for many years. Generally, the snails are tucked into their pretty cornucopia shells along with a generous concoction of heavenly, garlicky butter. They are heated until they are sizzling hot and the butter oozes all over the little snail plates, making it easy to sop up the excess with slices of fresh crusty French bread. The Red Lion Inn has its own take on this delectable dish, serving it with mushrooms in puff pastry shells.

4 frozen puff pastry shells
$\frac{1}{2}$ cup Escargot Butter (see recipe below)
28 canned escargots, drained
8-10 fresh button mushrooms, cleaned and sliced
1 cup heavy cream
4 tablespoons chopped fresh parsley

1. Bake the pastry shells according to package directions. Keep warm.

2. Place the prepared *Escargot Butter,* snails, and mushrooms in a sauté pan over medium heat and cook until the butter has melted, stirring occasionally.

3. Add the cream and 2 tablespoons of the parsley, mixing thoroughly. Simmer, stirring occasionally, until the sauce has thickened, about 20 minutes.

4. Spoon the snails and mushrooms into the warm pastry shells and pour the sauce over them. Garnish with the remaining parsley.

SERVES 4

Escargot Butter
$\frac{1}{2}$ cup butter, at room temperature
2 teaspoons minced garlic
2 teaspoons minced onions

4. Place the salt pork in a heavy pot and sauté until partially rendered, about 5 minutes. Be careful, this will splatter. (Or, melt the margarine in a heavy pot.)

5. Remove the pork from the pot and set aside. Remove half of the melted fat. Sauté the onions in the remaining fat over medium heat until translucent but not brown, about 5 minutes.

6. Add the flour to the onions and blend thoroughly to make a roux. Cook over medium heat, stirring constantly, for 5-6 minutes. (If you prefer a thicker chowder, more flour may be added.)

7. Add all of the reserved broth to the roux and stir until hot and smooth. Stir in the potatoes, clams, remaining fat, milk, and cream. Adjust the seasonings and add the butter just before serving, stirring until melted. Serve.

SERVES 10

"The dining room is the heart and soul of a hotel. It must be agreeable in all its appointments. In color, in size, in outlook, in furnishing. The dining room at Plumb's [later The Red Lion Inn] invited entrance, inspired appetite; it was a pleasant place."

— *The Pittsfield Sun*, September 3, 1896

Roasted Corn Chowder

¹/₄ pound bacon, diced
3 ears fresh corn, shucked and kernels cut from cobs
4 stalks celery, diced
1 medium onion, diced
1 small leek, diced
1 medium baking potato, peeled and diced
4 cups chicken stock or canned chicken broth
4 sprigs fresh thyme, rinsed and diced
2 cups milk
salt and black pepper to taste

1. Fry the bacon in a large pot until limp. Add the corn, celery, onion, leek, and potato and gently cook over medium heat until the vegetables are tender, about 6-8 minutes.

2. Add the stock and thyme and bring to a simmer. Gently simmer for 10 minutes.

3. Add the milk, salt, and black pepper and bring to a simmer. Serve hot.

SERVES 6-8

"Hot soup at table is very vulgar; it either leads to an unseemly mode of taking it, or keeps people waiting too long whilst it cools. Soup should be brought to table only moderately warm."

— *Hints on Etiquette*, 1844

7. Pour the soup into individual ovenproof crocks and top each serving with a slice of the prepared bread. Sprinkle with the remaining cheese and broil just until the cheese is bubbly, lightly browned, and crusted on top. Serve immediately.

SERVES 10-12

"Aunt Mert approved original design for sign, but Uncle Charles opposed on the grounds that the lion was too thin and might reflect on his table."

— notation in The Red Lion Inn's
guest book, May 1936

Hearty Split Pea Soup

This thrifty, peasant-style soup is excellent as a meal by itself, perhaps served with a crusty French bread, a salad, and a bottle of wine.

Stock:
1 tablespoon olive oil
1 large onion, diced
1 ¹/₂ stalks celery, diced
¹/₂ large carrot, diced
2 smoked ham hocks (about 1 pound each), cut in half
1 bay leaf
3 quarts cold water

Soup:
1 tablespoon olive oil
1 large onion, diced
1 stalk celery, diced
¹/₂ large carrot, diced
1 pound bag dried green split peas (2 cups)
3 quarts prepared stock (see Stock above)
ground cumin to taste
salt and black pepper to taste

1. For the stock: Heat the oil in a large pot. Add all of the vegetables, cover, and over medium heat, allow condensation to form until the vegetable juices are extracted.

2. Add the halved ham hocks and sauté over medium heat until the vegetables are soft, about 5 minutes. Add the bay leaf and cold water and simmer gently until the meat and vegetables are very soft, about 2 hours 30 minutes.

3. Strain the stock through a fine sieve, retaining the liquid and discarding the vegetable pulp and ham. Makes about 3 quarts.

4. For the soup: Heat the oil in a large pot. Add all of the diced vegetables and sauté until the vegetables begin to soften. Add the dried peas and the prepared stock and simmer over medium heat until the peas are soft, about 30 minutes. Season with the cumin, salt, and black pepper. Serve hot with *Homemade Croutons* (recipe following).

SERVES 8-10

Homemade Croutons

The Red Lion Inn uses these croutons as a garnish on salads, as well as soups.

5 slices day-old bread or dinner rolls, cut into ¹/₂" cubes
¹/₂ teaspoon garlic salt
¹/₂ teaspoon ground basil
¹/₂ teaspoon ground oregano
¹/₂ cup clarified butter, melted

1. Preheat oven to 350° F.
2. Spread the bread cubes on a large sheet pan.
3. Combine the garlic and herbs in a small bowl and sprinkle over the bread cubes.
4. Ladle the butter over the cubes and bake for 15 minutes. Stir the croutons and continue baking and turning until the croutons are golden brown on all sides. Watch carefully, as they burn easily. Allow to cool.
5. Store the croutons in an airtight container until ready to use. The croutons will keep for about 1 week.

YIELD 5 CUPS

To make clarified butter: Dice 1 pound of unsalted butter and place in a double boiler over very low heat, keeping the water warm, but not hot. Let the butter melt gently. Do not stir. Remove from heat and allow to stand until the butter separates and the solids fall to the bottom, about 40-50 minutes. Gently pour the clear liquid on top through a piece of doubled cheesecloth into a container. Excess clarified butter can be stored in a covered container in the refrigerator for several weeks, cutting off portions as needed. Clarified butter does not burn as easily as whole butter and is ideal for use in sauces or for sautéing and roasting delicate meats and fish.

Cold Strawberry Soup

This recipe is a favorite at The Red Lion Inn throughout the summer months.

3 cups fresh or frozen strawberries
$\frac{1}{4}$ teaspoon ground cinnamon
$\frac{1}{4}$ teaspoon salt
4 ounces frozen orange juice concentrate
$\frac{1}{2}$ cup water
$\frac{1}{4}$ cup red burgundy wine
pinch ground cloves
1 $\frac{1}{2}$ tablespoons cornstarch
1 $\frac{1}{2}$ tablespoons water
1 pint vanilla ice cream
2 cups light cream
6-8 fresh whole strawberries, for garnish

1. Combine the strawberries, cinnamon, salt, orange juice, water, wine, and cloves in a large saucepan and bring to a boil over medium heat. Reduce heat and simmer for 10-12 minutes.

2. Mix together the cornstarch and water in a small bowl, Stir $\frac{1}{4}$ cup of the strawberry mixture into the cornstarch mixture, then return the combined mixture to the soup. Bring to a boil and stir until thickened, about 5 minutes. Allow to cool.

3. Add the ice cream and light cream and stir until the ice cream has melted. Refrigerate for 1 hour. Garnish each serving with a fresh strawberry. Serve.

SERVES 6-8

Smoked Chicken Salad with Warm Chutney Dressing

4 cups washed and shredded red or green leaf lettuce
8 cups washed and torn spinach leaves
2 cups washed and shredded radicchio leaves
³/₄ pound smoked chicken, cut into small pieces
³/₄ pound extra-sharp cheddar cheese, sliced ¹/₄" thick
12 slices apple, unpeeled and cored
12 tomato wedges
¹/₂ cup Warm Chutney Dressing (see recipe below)

1. Divide and center the lettuce among 4 plates. Pile the spinach on top of the lettuce to create a mound.

2. Sprinkle the radicchio over all, then arrange the chicken pieces in the center of the greens. Fan the cheese slices around the chicken. Arrange the apple slices and tomato wedges, alternating around the edge of each plate.

3. Pour the prepared *Warm Chutney Dressing* over all and serve immediately.

SERVES 4

Warm Chutney Dressing

³/₄ cup prepared chutney
1 ¹/₄ cups corn oil
2 tablespoons bacon fat
¹/₄ cup cider vinegar
1 tablespoon light brown sugar
2 tablespoons crisply cooked and chopped bacon

Combine all of the ingredients in a saucepan and heat over medium heat. Cook, stirring frequently, until thoroughly blended and heated.

YIELD 2 CUPS

Spinach & Bacon Salad

4 Red Delicious apples, unpeeled and sliced
8 cups washed and torn spinach leaves
2 cups sliced fresh mushrooms
8 thin slices red onion
$1/2$ cup Warm Chutney Dressing (see recipe on page 50)
12 slices bacon, crisply cooked and crumbled

1. Place one-fourth of the apple slices on each of 4 salad plates. Pile the spinach on top of the apples and garnish with the mushroom and onion slices.

2. Spoon the prepared *Warm Chutney Dressing* over all and scatter the bacon on top. Serve immediately.

SERVES 4

DATE	NAME	ADDRESS
10/2x/98	Dionne Warwick	THANK you for making my STAY So EASY. I love the FireHouse, When I come back just for "R&R" this Has to Be where I stay.

Dionne Warwick penned this note of thanks in The Red Lion's guest register.

Red Lion Inn Potato Salad

1 pound red-skinned potatoes, unpeeled and cut into 6 pieces
$^1/_4$ medium red onion, minced
3 sprigs fresh tarragon, rinsed and chopped
1 tablespoon whole grain mustard
$^1/_3$ cup mayonnaise
salt and black pepper to taste

1. Steam the potatoes in a steamer until tender when tested with a knife, about 12-14 minutes. Allow to cool.

2. Combine the cooled potatoes, onion, tarragon, mustard, and mayonnaise in a bowl and mix together well. Add the salt and black pepper and chill in the refrigerator until ready to serve.

SERVES 4

"A salad is a sort of mealtime magician, able to jump in and supply the contrasts that make meals sparkle."

— The General Foods Cookbook, 1959

Red Lion Inn Four-Bean Salad

This salad and dressing should be started the day before you plan to serve it, to allow time for the beans to soak and the dressing flavors to meld.

$\frac{1}{2}$ cup dried chickpeas
$\frac{1}{2}$ cup dried red kidney beans
$\frac{1}{2}$ cup dried black beans
$\frac{1}{2}$ cup dried white kidney beans
$\frac{1}{4}$ cup diced Spanish onions
$\frac{1}{2}$ cup diced celery
$\frac{1}{2}$ cup diced canned pimientos
$\frac{1}{2}$ cup Red Lion Inn Robust Italian Dressing (see recipe on page 56)
salt and black pepper to taste
1 tablespoon chopped fresh parsley

1. Rinse the beans in a strainer and remove any impurities. In separate bowls, soak the chickpeas and each type of the beans overnight (minimum 4 hours) in water to cover by 2". (Or, bring each to a boil in separate saucepans and simmer for 2 minutes. Remove from heat and set aside to soak for 1 $\frac{1}{2}$ hours.)

2. Combine the beans, with the soaking water, in a large pot, placing the chickpeas in a separate saucepan. Bring the beans and the chickpeas to a boil. Reduce heat and simmer until tender, about 1 hour. Do not overcook. Watch closely, as the chickpeas will be cooked before the beans. Remove from heat, drain, and allow to cool.

3. Combine the beans and chickpeas in a large bowl. Add the onions, celery, and pimientos. Stir in the prepared *Red Lion Inn Robust Italian Dressing* and toss until the ingredients are well covered. Season with the salt and black pepper and sprinkle with the parsley. Place in the refrigerator, covered, for at least 4 hours before serving. Serve.

SERVES 10-12

Coleslaw

A coleslaw of shredded cabbage and shredded carrots is a popular Red Lion Inn accompaniment to luncheon and dinner dishes, especially fish.

2 cups finely grated green cabbage
1 cup finely grated carrots
$^1/_2$ cup Coleslaw Dressing (see recipe below)

    1. Combine the cabbage and carrots in a bowl.
    2. Toss the vegetables with the prepared *Coleslaw Dressing* and serve.

SERVES 6

Coleslaw Dressing

2 cups mayonnaise
6 tablespoons pure maple syrup
4 tablespoons white vinegar
2 teaspoons ground paprika
4 tablespoons light cream

Combine all of the ingredients in a bowl and mix well. This dressing will keep in the refrigerator for 2-3 days.

YIELD 2 $^1/_2$ CUPS

Aunt Zoa's Cranberry-Apple Jelly Salad

Aunt Zoa was Jane Fitzpatrick's beloved sister, friend, companion, and also the business manager for Country Curtains. This recipe was one that she often contributed to family gatherings.

1 cup unpeeled, cored, and sectioned McIntosh apples
1 cup fresh cranberries
1 cup sugar
1 package lemon gelatin
1 cup hot water
1 cup pineapple juice
½ cup halved and seeded Tokay grapes
¼ cup chopped walnuts
1 cup canned crushed pineapple, drained
1 cup heavy cream
1 teaspoon sugar
8-10 fresh lettuce leaves, rinsed

1. Grind the apples and cranberries in a food grinder or a food processor. Stir in the 1 cup sugar and let stand for 10 minutes.

2. Combine the gelatin and the hot water in a large bowl and stir until the gelatin is dissolved. Add the pineapple juice. Chill in the refrigerator until the gelatin has reached the soft-set stage, about 30-60 minutes.

3. Add the ground apples and cranberries, the grapes, walnuts, and crushed pineapple to the gelatin, mixing well. Pour into individual molds (or one large mold) and return to the refrigerator to fully set.

4. Whip the cream in a bowl until creamy. Add the 1 teaspoon sugar and continue whipping until soft peaks form. Do not overwhip. Place each serving on a lettuce leaf and top with a dollop of the whipped cream. Serve.

SERVES 8-10

Red Lion Inn Robust Italian Dressing

This classic salad dressing is a versatile one. It is excellent on a variety of salads and can be used as a marinade for steaks, chicken, and lamb kabobs.

3 cloves garlic, minced
4 tablespoons minced red onions
2 tablespoons minced fresh parsley
3 tablespoons minced red bell pepper
2 tablespoons dried basil
1 ¹/₂ tablespoons garlic powder
1 tablespoon dried oregano
2 teaspoons crushed black peppercorns
¹/₈ teaspoon cayenne pepper
1 teaspoon salt
¹/₄ teaspoon ground mustard
1 cup red wine vinegar
3 cups olive oil

   1. Place the garlic, onions, parsley, and bell pepper in a bowl and add all of the herbs, spices, and seasonings. Mix together well.

   2. Stir in the vinegar and allow the dressing to stand for 10 minutes.

   3. Whisk in the oil. Adjust the seasonings, cover, and refrigerate for 24 hours to meld the flavors.

YIELD 4 CUPS

Red Lion Inn Russian Dressing

Two traditional salad dressings in particular generate many recipe requests at The Red Lion Inn: *Red Lion Inn Russian Dressing* and *Red Lion Inn Blue Cheese Dressing.* Enjoy!

1 hard-boiled egg (optional)
2 sweet pickles
1 tablespoon chopped onions
2 teaspoons chopped red bell pepper
$^1/_2$ small green bell pepper, cored, seeded, and quartered
$^1/_2$ clove garlic, peeled
1 cup mayonnaise
$^1/_4$ cup chili sauce
$^1/_4$ teaspoon Worcestershire sauce
salt and black pepper to taste
$^1/_4$ teaspoon Tabasco sauce

Process the egg, pickles, onions, both bell peppers, and garlic together in a food processor. Add the remaining ingredients and mix well. This dressing will keep in the refrigerator for 1 week.

YIELD 2 CUPS

Red Lion Inn Blue Cheese Dressing

$^1/_2$ cup crumbled blue cheese
$^1/_2$ cup sour cream
1 cup mayonnaise
$^1/_4$ cup buttermilk
1 tablespoon water
2 teaspoons white vinegar
$^1/_8$ teaspoon Tabasco sauce
salt and black pepper to taste

Place $^1/_4$ cup of the blue cheese in a bowl. Add the other ingredients and mix well. Add the remaining blue cheese and stir gently. This dressing will keep in the refrigerator for up to 10 days.

YIELD 2 CUPS

The Red Lion Inn's birdcage collection in the courtyard.

MIMI L. MACDONALD

Ranch Dressing

At The Red Lion Inn, this dressing is used for several dishes — over a tossed salad, in place of mayonnaise in chicken sandwiches, and also in bacon, lettuce, and tomato sandwiches.

2 ¹/₂ cups mayonnaise
¹/₂ cup sour cream
¹/₂ cup buttermilk
1 ¹/₂ tablespoons garlic powder
2 ¹/₂ tablespoons dried chives
dash salt
dash white pepper
1 drop Tabasco sauce

Combine all of the ingredients in a bowl and mix well. Refrigerate, covered, for at least 1 hour to allow the flavors to meld.

YIELD 3 ¹/₂ CUPS

> *"Ate well but not wisely"*
>
> — Frank Crowninshield, entry in
> The Red Lion Inn's guest book,
> October 11, 1941

CHAPTER 6

Breads & Muffins

In early New England, young girls learned to make bread just as their brothers learned to tend the plow. Bread was an essential part of a Colonial meal. Having learned from her failure to make corn flour act just like wheat and rye flours, the New England housewife created distinctive breads of her own. Corn bread and brown bread bore little resemblance to the light, airy white breads of the old country, but were nevertheless suitable accompaniments to Colonial dinners.

According to Root and de Rochemont, who must have read thousands of old cookbooks while researching their 1976 book *Eating in America, A History,* Mrs. J. Chadwick offered some pearls of wisdom about bread in her 1853 book *Home Cookery:* "Until the end of the eighteenth century, the only way to make baked goods light was to beat air into the dough, along with eggs, or to add yeast (but it had to be natural yeast, made by the cook) or spirits. Then, in the 1790s, pearlash was discovered

in America. Produced by burning wood, pearlash was responsible for some of the wholesale destruction of American forests, but it revolutionized baking methods.

"Pearlash is potassium carbonate; it produces carbon dioxide in baking dough and makes it rise. The fledgling American republic exported some 8,000 tons of pearlash to Europe in 1792."

It was not until the 1850s that baking powder, which worked exactly as pearlash, except that it was new and improved, was commercially produced. In 1857, Professor E.N. Horsford of Harvard developed a formula for phosphate baking powder that moved a writer in *Practical Housekeeping* to declare, "Horsford's 'Bread Preparation' is superior to yeast or soda."

Quick breads, made with baking powder instead of yeast, were another way to use the abundance of New England harvests to advantage, and The Red Lion Inn has developed its own delightful versions, many of which are shared here.

Pineapple Bread

When New England sailing captains left the tropics of Polynesia to begin their return voyage, they often brought cases of pineapples with them. On their arrival home, the plump, juicy pineapples would be placed on the gatepost, signaling the safe return of the captain and inviting friends in to celebrate with the family. This sign of "Open House" has been the symbol of hospitality ever since.

¹/₂ cup butter, at room temperature
1 cup sugar
2 eggs
2 cups flour
1 teaspoon baking powder
pinch salt
1 cup canned crushed pineapple, drained
¹/₂ cup chopped walnuts

1. Preheat oven to 350° F. Grease and flour two 9" x 5" loaf pans.
2. Cream together the butter and sugar in a large mixing bowl. Beat in the eggs, one at a time, and cream well after each addition.
3. Sift together the flour, baking powder, and salt in a bowl. Add the flour mixture alternately with the crushed pineapple to the egg mixture. Stir in the walnuts.
4. Pour the batter into the prepared pans and bake for 45-60 minutes, or until a toothpick inserted in the center comes out clean.

YIELD 2 LOAVES

Red Lion Inn Lemon Bread

The Red Lion Inn's *Lemon Bread* is justifiably renowned. At lunch and dinner, the bread is served in a basket along with yeast rolls, offering a sweet alternative to traditional dinner rolls.

³/₄ cup margarine
2 cups sugar
3 eggs
1 egg yolk
3 ¹/₃ cups flour
1 tablespoon plus ¹/₂ teaspoon baking powder
1 ¹/₂ teaspoons salt
2 cups Lemon Pudding (see recipe below), or use packaged mix or canned
3 tablespoons milk

1. Preheat oven to 350° F. Grease two 9" x 5" loaf pans.
2. Cream together well the margarine and sugar in a large bowl. Add the eggs and egg yolk, one at a time, mixing well after each addition.
3. Sift together the dry ingredients and add to the egg mixture. Add the prepared *Lemon Pudding* and milk and mix until very well blended.
4. Pour the batter into the prepared pans and bake for 40-50 minutes, or until a toothpick inserted in the center comes out clean.

YIELD 2 LOAVES

Lemon Pudding

3 tablepoons cornstarch
1 cup sugar
dash salt
1 ¹/₂ cups warm water
¹/₂ cup fresh lemon juice
4 egg yolks, beaten
1 tablespoon butter

1. Stir together the cornstarch, sugar, and salt in a heavy saucepan. Add the water and lemon juice and cook over medium heat, stirring constantly, until the mixture comes to a boil.

2. Stir a small amount of the lemon mixture into the egg yolks, then add the yolks to the saucepan. Cook, but do not boil, until thick, about 6-8 minutes, stirring vigorously to retain a smooth consistency. Remove from heat.

3. Stir the butter into the lemon mixture until melted. Cover and allow to cool. The pudding will thicken more as it cools.

YIELD 2 $^1/_2$ CUPS

"The Red Lion, at Stockbridge, made us welcome, and after Mr. Mears and I had gone to our rooms and bathed and dressed, we met in the lobby and went in to dinner. He requested milk toast 'and a can of sardines, unopened, but be sure to bring me the key.'

Evidently, the Red Lion staff is accustomed to visitors of great peculiarity or else had dealt with Mr. Mears before, because no one so much as lifted an eyebrow. Mr. Mears dumped the sardines onto the milk toast, stirred the mixture into a sort of paste, and ate it mechanically. I had a steak dinner, which I enjoyed very much, having developed a technique for the occasion. My technique consisted simply of not looking at Mr. Mears any more than I could help. . . ."

— James Reid Parker,
The New Yorker, September 4, 1948

Cranberry-Orange Nut Bread

The Pilgrims found cranberries growing wild when they arrived in their new country, and they immediately began adapting them to various uses. Massachusetts is still the cranberry capital, and this recipe is a delightful way to use this typically New England crop.

4 cups flour
2 cups sugar
1 teaspoon baking soda
1 tablespoon baking powder
2 teaspoons salt
$^1/_2$ cup margarine
1 $^1/_2$ cups fresh orange juice
2 tablespoons grated orange peel
2 eggs, beaten
1 cup chopped walnuts
4 cups chopped fresh cranberries

1. Preheat oven to 375° F. Grease two 9" x 5" loaf pans.

2. Sift together all of the dry ingredients in a large bowl. Cut in the margarine, using a pastry blender, until the mixture resembles small peas.

3. Mix together the orange juice, orange peel, and eggs in a bowl, then combine the egg mixture with the flour mixture, stirring well. Fold in the walnuts and cranberries.

4. Pour the batter into the prepared pans and bake for 1 hour, or until a toothpick inserted in the center comes out clean. Allow the loaves to cool in the pans, then wrap the loaves in plastic wrap and let rest overnight (this improves the flavor and makes slicing easier).

YIELD 2 LOAVES

Orange Bread

1 medium orange, peeled and seeded
$^2/_3$ cup dates, pits removed
$^1/_2$ cup halved walnuts
2 tablespoons butter
$^1/_2$ cup warm water
1 egg
2 cups flour
1 $^1/_2$ teaspoons baking powder
$^1/_4$ teaspoon baking soda
$^1/_4$ teaspoon salt
$^3/_4$ cup sugar

1. Preheat oven to 350° F. Grease one 9" x 5" loaf pan.

2. Grind the orange pulp, dates, and walnuts in a food grinder or food processor. Set aside.

3. Whip together the butter, water, and egg in a large bowl. Sift together all of the dry ingredients and add to the egg mixture. Blend together well. Add the reserved date mixture and combine thoroughly.

4. Pour the batter into the prepared pan and bake for 40-50 minutes, or until a toothpick inserted in the center comes out clean.

YIELD 1 LOAF

Apricot Nut Bread

1 cup dried apricot halves
1 cup fresh orange juice
$^1/_4$ cup butter or margarine
$^3/_4$ cup sugar
1 egg
$^1/_2$ cup milk
1 cup whole bran cereal
2 teaspoons grated orange peel
$^1/_4$ cup slivered blanched almonds (see page 26)
2 cups flour
1 tablespoon baking powder
$^1/_2$ teaspoon baking soda
$^1/_2$ teaspoon salt

1. Preheat oven to 325° F. Grease one 9" x 5" loaf pan.

2. Dice the apricots into $^1/_4$" pieces. Combine the apricots and orange juice in a saucepan and cook over moderately low heat until the mixture comes to a boil. Continue cooking for 5 minutes. Remove from heat and allow to cool.

3. Cream together the butter and sugar in a large bowl. Add the egg and milk and mix until well blended. Stir in the cereal, orange peel, cooled apricot mixture, and almonds and mix together well.

4. Sift together the flour, baking powder, baking soda, and salt. Add the flour mixture to the apricot mixture and stir until thoroughly moistened.

5. Pour the batter into the prepared pan and bake for 55-60 minutes, or until a toothpick inserted in the center comes out clean.

YIELD 1 LOAF

Pumpkin Bread or Muffins

The pumpkin was one of the earliest vegetables that the Pilgrims learned to grow. This form of squash was a plentiful Indian crop that apparently did not generate love at first sight. An early saying went: "We have pumpkins at morning, and pumpkins at noon; if it were not for pumpkins we should be undoon." Nevertheless, this recipe, served often at The Red Lion Inn, is a delicious use for that ageless crop. It works equally well as loaves or muffins.

4 eggs
2 ¹/₃ cups sugar
1 cup vegetable oil
2 cups canned pumpkin
3 cups flour
¹/₂ teaspoon salt
1 ³/₄ teaspoons baking soda
2 ³/₄ teaspoons ground cinnamon
¹/₂ teaspoon ground nutmeg
¹/₂ teaspoon ground cloves
¹/₄ teaspoon ground allspice
1 cup chopped walnuts
¹/₃ cup golden raisins
¹/₄ cup sugar, for topping
1 teaspoon ground cinnamon, for topping

1. Preheat oven to 375° F. Grease two 9" x 5" loaf pans or 24 muffin cups.

2. Combine the eggs, the 2 ¹/₃ cups sugar, the oil, and pumpkin in a large bowl and stir until smooth.

3. Sift together the dry ingredients and spices in a bowl. Add the walnuts, raisins, and flour mixture to the egg mixture and mix thoroughly. Pour the batter into the prepared pans or muffin cups.

4. Mix together the ¹/₄ cup sugar and the 1 teaspoon cinnamon in a small bowl and sprinkle over the batter.

5. Bake the bread for 1 hour 10 minutes or the muffins for 35-40 minutes, or until a toothpick inserted in the center comes out clean.

YIELD 2 LOAVES OR 24 MUFFINS

Apple Cider Bread or Muffins

The flavor of the baked bread will improve if the bread is allowed to rest for 24 hours.

1 cup butter
1 ¼ cups sugar
3 eggs
4 cups flour
1 ½ tablespoons baking powder
1 ½ teaspoons salt
1 ½ teaspoons ground cinnamon
2 cups apple cider
2 cups peeled, cored, and chopped apples
¼ cup sugar, for topping
1 teaspoon ground cinnamon

1. Preheat oven to 375° F. Grease two 9" x 5" loaf pans or 18 muffin cups.

2. Cream together the butter and 1 ¼ cups sugar in a large bowl. Add the eggs, one at a time, and cream well after each addition.

3. Sift together the flour, baking powder, salt, and cinnamon in a bowl. Add the flour mixture to the egg mixture, alternating with the cider. Stir in the apples.

4. Pour the batter into the prepared pans or muffin cups. Combine the ¼ cup sugar with the cinnamon in a small bowl. Sprinkle the cinnamon mixture over the batter and bake for 50-70 minutes for the bread or 30-40 minutes for the muffins, or until a toothpick inserted in the center comes out clean.

YIELD 2 LOAVES OR 18 MUFFINS

> *"To make good bread or to understand the process of making it is the duty of every woman; indeed an art that should never be neglected in the education of a lady. The lady derives her title from 'dividing or distributing bread'; the more perfect the bread the more perfect the lady."*
>
> — Mrs. Sara Hale,
> *Receipts for the Millions*, 1857

Banana Nut Bread or Muffins

Bananas were introduced to America by New England sea captain, Lorenzo Baker of Wellfleet, Massachusetts. He first brought back only one bunch of green bananas from Jamaica, but they were so well received that he eventually gave up seafaring and went into the banana business full-time.

³/₄ cup butter
1 ³/₄ cups sugar
3 eggs
1 egg yolk
5 large ripe bananas, peeled and mashed
3 ¹/₂ cups flour
1 ¹/₂ teaspoons salt
1 tablespoon plus 1 teaspoon baking powder
¹/₂ cup chopped walnuts

1. Preheat oven to 350° F. Grease two 9" x 5" loaf pans or 18 muffin cups.

2. Cream together the butter and sugar in a large bowl. Beat in all of the eggs, one at a time, creaming well after each addition.

3. Mix the mashed bananas into the egg mixture (the batter will appear to "break" and become soupy).

4. Sift together the flour, salt, and baking powder in a bowl and add to the egg mixture. Mix gently to combine. Stir in the walnuts.

5. Pour the batter into the prepared pans or muffin cups and bake the bread for 50-60 minutes or the muffins for 25-30 minutes, or until a toothpick inserted in the center comes out clean.

YIELD 2 LOAVES OR 18 MUFFINS

Blueberry Muffins

New Englanders have an enduring devotion to blueberry muffins, as this passage in *The American Heritage Cookbook* illustrates: "In 1894, recalling a breakfast in Boston that he had had some years earlier with Oliver Wendell Holmes's publisher, James T. Fields, William Dean Howells wrote, 'I remember his burlesque pretence that morning of an inextinguishable grief when I owned that I had never eaten blueberry cake [muffins] before, and how he kept returning to the pathos of the fact that there should be a region of the earth where blueberry cake was unknown.'"

³/₄ cup margarine, at room temperature
³/₄ cup sugar
2 eggs
3 cups flour
1 tablespoon baking powder
1 teaspoon salt
1 ¹/₃ cups milk
1 cup fresh or frozen blueberries

1. Preheat oven to 375° F. Grease 12 muffin cups.

2. Beat the margarine with ¹/₂ cup sugar in a large bowl until well blended. Add the eggs, one at a time, creaming thoroughly after each addition, until light and fluffy.

3. Combine 2 ²/₃ cups of the flour with the remaining dry ingredients in a bowl. Add the flour mixture to the egg mixture, then add the milk. Mix just until moist. Do not overmix.

4. Place the remaining flour in a plastic bag. Add the berries and shake until the berries are lightly coated with the flour. Add the berries to the batter. (The batter will be very stiff if the berries are frozen.)

5. Fill the prepared muffin cups two-thirds full. Sprinkle the ¹/₄ cup sugar over the tops and bake for 20-30 minutes, or until a toothpick inserted in the center comes out clean.

YIELD 12 MUFFINS

Bran Muffins

These popular bran muffins are a distinctive addition to The Red Lion Inn's repertoire. The batter should be prepared the night before you're going to bake the muffins.

$^1/_2$ cup margarine
1 cup sugar
2 eggs, beaten
2 $^3/_4$ cups flour
2 cups buttermilk
2 $^1/_2$ teaspoons baking soda
1 cup hot water
1 cup bran flakes
2 cups All-Bran cereal
1 $^1/_4$ cups finely grated carrots
$^1/_2$ cup raisins

1. Cream together the margarine and sugar in a large bowl. Add the eggs, one at a time, and cream well after each addition.

2. Sift the flour, then add the flour to the egg mixture, alternating with the buttermilk, mixing well after each addition.

3. Dissolve the baking soda in the water. Add to the batter and mix well. Stir in the bran flakes and cereal. The batter will be rather thin. Let stand, covered, in the refrigerator overnight.

4. Preheat oven to 350° F. Grease 18 muffin cups.

5. Just before baking, add the carrots and raisins to the batter. Pour the batter into the prepared muffin cups and bake for 30-40 minutes, or until a toothpick inserted in the center comes out clean. Allow to cool for 10 minutes before removing from cups.

YIELD 18 MUFFINS

Cheese Bread or Cloverleaf Cheese Rolls

¹/₄ cup butter
1 cup diced onions
1 ¹/₂ cups milk
2 tablespoons dry yeast
1 tablespoon salt
¹/₂ cup sugar
¹/₂ cup warm water
2 eggs
6 cups flour
2 cups grated extra-sharp cheddar cheese
2 tablespoons butter, melted

1. Grease two 9" x 5" loaf pans or 24 muffin cups.

2. Melt the butter in a saucepan and sauté the onions over medium heat until soft, about 5 minutes. Stir in the milk and allow the mixture to cool.

3. Combine the yeast, salt, sugar, and warm water (should register about 105° on a candy thermometer) in a large bowl. Stir well and set aside until the yeast has formed foamy bubbles on top, about 10 minutes.

4. Stir the cooled onion mixture and the eggs into the yeast mixture. Add the flour and cheese and mix thoroughly. Place the dough on a floured surface and knead until it is no longer sticky and has some elasticity, about 5-10 minutes. Place the dough in a greased stainless steel bowl, turning once to coat. Cover with plastic wrap and set in a warm, draft-free place. Let rise until doubled in size, about 1 hour 30 minutes.

5. Punch down the dough. Place on a lightly floured surface and knead briefly to release the air bubbles. Divide the dough in half and shape each half into a loaf. Place in the prepared loaf pans, cover with plastic wrap, and allow to rise again until the bread fills the loaf pans, about 45 minutes. (For rolls, shape the dough into small balls so that 3 small balls will fit into the bottom of each muffin cup. Cover with plastic wrap and allow to rise until doubled in size.)

6. Preheat oven to 350° F. Brush the tops of the loaves with some of the melted butter and bake until golden brown and the loaves sound hollow when tapped, about 40-45 minutes. (For rolls, bake until golden brown, about 10-12 minutes.) Remove the pans from the oven and immediately brush the bread with the remaining melted butter. Allow to cool in the pans for 10 minutes before turning out. Cool on wire racks.

YIELD 2 LOAVES OR 24 ROLLS

French Bread or Knotted French Rolls

1 cup lukewarm water
1 tablespoon dry yeast
1 tablespoon sugar
1 1/4 teaspoons salt
2 tablespoons vegetable oil

3 cups flour
2 tablespoons cornmeal
1 cup hot water
1 1/2 teaspoons cornstarch

1. Grease a sheet pan.

2. Whisk together the lukewarm water, yeast, sugar, salt, and oil in a large bowl. Add 1 1/2 cups of the flour and beat until blended. Gather the dough into a ball.

3. Knead the dough on a floured surface, adding the remaining flour until all is well blended, about 10 minutes. The dough should be pliable and elastic.

4. Place the dough in a greased stainless steel bowl, turning once to coat, and cover with plastic wrap. Let rise in a warm, draft-free place until doubled in size, about 1 hour.

5. Punch down the dough, return to the bowl, cover with plastic wrap, and let rise until doubled in size again, about 30 minutes.

6. Divide the dough in half and let rise for 10 minutes. Press each portion out flat and roll up jelly roll-style to form a long loaf. Sprinkle the greased sheet pan with the cornmeal and place the loaves on the cornmeal. Let rise, covered with plastic wrap, until doubled in size, about 20-30 minutes.

7. Preheat oven to 450° F. Combine the hot water with the cornstarch in a saucepan and heat for 1-2 minutes, stirring constantly. Allow to cool to room temperature.

8. Score diagonal cuts on the tops of the loaves with a sharp knife and brush with some of the cornstarch mixture. Place the sheet pan with the loaves in the oven and place a shallow pan of water on the rack below the sheet pan. Bake for 10 minutes. Brush the loaves with the cornstarch mixture again and bake until the loaves sound hollow when tapped, about 25 minutes.

9. For rolls: After the dough has been divided in half (see step 6.) and has rested, divide each half into 12 sections. Roll each section into a 5" rope and tie each rope into a knot. Let rise. Preheat oven to 450° F. Bake until golden brown, about 10-12 minutes, brushing with the cornstarch mixture halfway through baking.

YIELD 2 LOAVES OR 24 ROLLS

Yeast Rolls

Although this recipe may easily be divided in half, it is best made in a larger quantity to retain the necessary sweetness.

These rolls will freeze beautifully, making them available for dinner at a moment's notice.

4 cups milk
3 tablespoons dry yeast
6 tablespoons sugar
¹/₂ teaspoon salt
6 cups flour
1 egg white
¹/₄ cup milk

1. Lightly grease a baking sheet.

2. Heat the milk in a saucepan over low heat until it reads 105° on a candy thermometer. Pour the hot milk into a large mixing bowl and sprinkle with the yeast. Stir well and set aside until the yeast has formed foamy bubbles on top, about 10 minutes.

3. Add the sugar and salt, then add 1 cup of the flour at a time, until a sticky dough is made. When too difficult to mix, add the remaining flour by kneading on a floured surface.

4. Place the dough in a large, greased stainless steel bowl, turning once to coat. Cover with plastic wrap and let rise in a warm, draft-free place until doubled in size, about 1 hour.

5. Punch down the dough and knead for a few minutes, just to release the air pockets. Cut or pull off small portions of the dough and roll each into a small ball (or roll each portion into a short rope and tie in a knot). Place the formed rolls on the prepared baking sheet and cover with plastic wrap. Let rise until doubled in size, about 18-20 minutes.

6. Preheat oven to 400° F. Prepare an egg wash by whipping together the egg white and milk in a small bowl. Brush the tops of the rolls with the egg wash and bake until golden brown, about 10-12 minutes.

7. To freeze the rolls: either freeze the raw dough or partially bake the rolls for about 8 minutes, then freeze. Finish baking the rolls just before serving.

YIELD 10 DOZEN ROLLS

Buttermilk Biscuits

2 ³/₄ cups flour
1 tablespoon plus 1 teaspoon baking powder
¹/₈ teaspoon salt
7 tablespoons butter
1 ¹/₄ cups buttermilk
1 egg
1 tablespoon water
2 tablespoons butter, melted

1. Preheat oven to 400° F.

2. Sift together the flour, baking powder, and salt in a bowl. Cut in the butter with a pastry blender or two knives until the mixture has the consistency of small peas.

3. Mix the buttermilk into the butter mixture with hands. Form the dough into a ball.

4. Roll out the dough to ¹/₂" thickness on a floured surface. Cut the biscuits out with a biscuit cutter and arrange on an ungreased baking sheet. Stir together the egg and water in a small bowl. Brush this egg wash on top of the biscuits and bake until golden brown, about 25-30 minutes.

5. Remove from the oven and brush the biscuits with the melted butter. Any of the biscuits not used immediately can be frozen.

YIELD 12 BISCUITS

"Papa didn't like baker's bread and I determined to learn to make homemade bread for him. It took all summer. Mixing was heavy work and baking a hot, hard chore. But there came a day when I took from the oven a perfect loaf, beautifully brown and light as a feather. I wrapped it in a snowy napkin and presented it to my father."

— New England Cookbook, 1954

Challah

1 package dry yeast
$^1/_4$ cup lukewarm water
3 tablespoons vegetable oil
1 tablepoon sugar
1 teaspoon salt
$^1/_3$ cup water, at room temperature
3 egg yolks, beaten
2 $^1/_4$ - 2 $^3/_4$ cups flour
1 egg yolk
2 tablespoons water

1. Grease a baking sheet.

2. Sprinkle the yeast over the $^1/_4$ cup lukewarm water in a large bowl. Stir well and set aside until the yeast has formed foamy bubbles on top, about 10 minutes.

3. Whisk in 2 tablespoons of the oil, the sugar, salt, and $^1/_3$ cup water. Add the 3 egg yolks. Using an electric mixer, beat the ingredients together. Add 1 $^1/_4$ cups of the flour and mix well.

4. Stir in enough additional flour to make the dough firm enough to handle, about $^3/_4$ cup. Let rest, covered, for 10 minutes. Knead the dough on a floured surface for 8-10 minutes, adding additional flour until the dough is smooth and shiny. Place the dough in a greased stainless steel bowl, turning once to coat. Cover with plastic wrap and let rise in a warm, draft-free place until doubled in size, about 40-60 minutes.

5. Divide the dough into thirds, cover with plastic wrap, and let rise for 10 minutes. With hands, roll the dough on a floured surface, forming 3 ropes of dough of equal length, about 18". Placing the ropes of dough on the prepared baking sheet, press all three together at the top and then braid them together.

6. Brush the braided loaf lightly with the remaining tablespoon of oil and let rise, covered with plastic wrap, for 30-40 minutes. (The bread will not double in size.)

7. Preheat oven to 375° F. Whisk together the 1 egg yolk and the 2 tablespoons of water in a small bowl to form an egg wash. Brush the loaf lightly with the mixture and bake until the loaf sounds hollow when tapped, about 25 minutes.

YIELD 1 LOAF

CHAPTER 7

Meat & Game

Meat is the star of American dinners. As Jean Anderson and Elaine Hanna say in *The New Doubleday Cookbook:* "It's the dish around which all others are planned, the one for which wines are chosen, the one that sets the tone of a meal. It's the most expensive part of our diet, the most universally well liked, the most versatile, and certainly one of the most nutritious. Meat thus deserves a worthy role and the best possible supporting cast. It needs skillful and imaginative handling, preferential treatment sometimes, and kid-glove care always."

Before beef, lamb, and pork were readily available to the Pilgrims in Colonial America, they depended on game for their dinner table. Wild turkeys, which roamed the New England countryside and are once again abundant in Berkshire fields, held a special place in American hearts — and still do. Benjamin Franklin once wrote to his daughter, Sarah Bache, "I wish the Bald Eagle had not been chose as the Representation of our Country; he is a Bird of bad moral Character, like those among men who live by sharpening and robbing, he is generally poor and often very lousy. . . . The turkey is. . . a much more respectable bird, and withal a true original Native of America."

The first cattle seem to have arrived in Florida in about 1550 and in Jamestown in 1611, but they were not plentiful. Early settlers did have an abundance of hogs, however, long before cattle ranches west of the cities were profitable enough to make beef a table staple — and they used every part of the animal in their cooking. They regularly used bacon, ham, roasts, chops, and spareribs. Housewives used the bones and ham hocks for soups, and they made their own sausage. They rendered the fat into lard and used it in pastries, breads, and cakes.

Only the rich, however, could afford fresh meat. But fresh poultry and game were available to even those New Englanders who lived in the country, and hogs cost nothing to keep, as they could forage for themselves. As early as 1640, Massachusetts was carrying on a profitable trade in salt pork.

In addition to pork, turkey, game birds, venison, and fish, early New Englanders devised a thrifty and easy dinner that enjoyed considerable popularity. Traditionally, a New England boiled dinner consists of boiled corned beef, cabbage, and other vegetables, served with a side dish of beets. Leftovers can be used for corned beef hash for breakfast the next day. If the meat is ground with the leftover beets, it will turn the hash a bright red, which the Pilgrims called Red Flannel Hash.

During the summer months, when the courtyard at The Red Lion Inn is open for dinner, Tuesday is Steak Night. That's the night when the outdoor grill is stoked, and steaks are cooked to order, accompanied by a salad bar. As the sun goes down and the tables are lit with candles in hurricane holders, it's a delightful place for a relaxing summer meal.

Note: See Chapter 13, Holiday Time at The Red Lion Inn, for the recipes *Roast Christmas Goose with Orange Gravy* and *Roast Turkey Red Lion Inn.*

"Sir, respect your dinner; idolize it, enjoy it properly. You will be by many hours in the week, many weeks in the year, and many years in your life the happier if you do."

— William Makepeace Thackeray, *Memorials of Gormandizing,* 1852

New England Boiled Dinner

When beef was finally available to early colonists, it was probably not particularly tender as it was generally stewed or pot roasted or corned. Corned beef, it should be pointed out, is made from a brisket or flank of beef, and it has nothing to do with corn. A corned beef is a piece of meat that has been submerged in a large stone crock of brine made with salt, sugar, and a little saltpeter. The size of the salt granules were about the size of English grain, or corn, and this seems to be where the name comes from.

1 corned beef brisket (4-5 pounds)
4 quarts chicken broth
1 teaspoon pickling spices
1 head garlic, unpeeled and cut into quarters
12 small new potatoes, peeled
6 carrots, coarsely chopped
6 small turnips, diced
8 small beets, with tops
hot mustard (optional)
prepared horseradish (optional)

1. Place the corned beef and broth in a Dutch oven. Add the pickling spices and garlic and bring to a boil over high heat. Reduce heat to low, cover, and simmer until the beef is cooked, about 3-3 hours 30 minutes.

2. Add the potatoes, carrots, and turnips to the pot and cook until the meat and vegetables are tender, about 30-45 minutes.

3. Meanwhile, cook the beets in a separate saucepan of boiling, salted water for 30-45 minutes (this prevents the beets from discoloring the other vegetables).

4. Remove the beef and all of the vegetables from their broth and arrange on a heated serving platter. Pass the mustard and horseradish, if desired.

SERVES 6-8

Roast Prime Rib of Beef

¹/₂ tablespoon salt
¹/₄ teaspoon black pepper
¹/₄ teaspoon white pepper
¹/₂ tablespoon dried thyme
¹/₂ tablespoon garlic powder
¹/₄ cup Worcestershire sauce
1 beef rib roast (9-10 pounds)
1 cup diced onions
¹/₄ cup diced carrots
¹/₄ cup diced celery
¹/₂ medium tomato, peeled and diced
3-4 sprigs fresh parsley, rinsed and chopped
1 cup beef broth

1. Combine the salt, black pepper, white pepper, thyme, and garlic powder in a small bowl.

2. Sprinkle the Worcestershire sauce over the roast. Then rub the salt mixture into the roast and let stand in the refrigerator for at least 3 hours.

3. One hour before cooking, remove the roast from the refrigerator and let it come to room temperature.

4. Preheat oven to 350° F.

5. Place the roast on a rack in a roasting pan. Surround the roast with the vegetables and parsley and bake until a meat thermometer registers 120°, about 45-60 minutes.

6. Remove the roast from the pan and let stand in a warm place, covered with aluminum foil, for 20-30 minutes before carving.

7. Meanwhile, drain the grease from the pan, leaving the vegetables in the pan. Add the beef broth, scraping with a spoon until all of the drippings are loosened. Simmer over medium heat on top of the stove for 10 minutes. Strain. Serve this *au jus* sauce as an accompaniment to the roast.

SERVES 8

Filet Mignon Red Lion Inn

¹/₂ cup vegetable oil
2 teaspoons Worcestershire sauce
salt and black pepper to taste
4 center-cut filet mignon (6-8 ounces each)
8 fresh mushroom caps, wiped clean
4 slices white bread, crusts removed
Béarnaise Sauce (see recipe below)

1. Preheat broiler.

2. Blend together ¹/₄ cup of the oil, Worcestershire sauce, salt, and black pepper in a small bowl. Place the steaks in a small casserole dish or on a pie plate. Pour the oil mixture over the steaks and marinate for 10 minutes, turning once. Drain, but reserve the marinade.

3. Transfer the steaks to the top of the broiler pan and broil for 6-8 minutes on the first side. Brush the steaks with the marinade, turn on the other side, and broil for 6 minutes (for medium rare).

4. Meanwhile, heat the remaining oil in a sauté pan. Add the mushroom caps and sauté over medium heat until tender, about 5 minutes, seasoning with salt and black pepper. Remove the mushroom caps from the pan and keep warm. Sauté the bread slices in the same pan until golden brown, about 5 minutes.

5. Place each cooked steak on a piece of sautéed bread. Spoon some of the prepared *Béarnaise Sauce* over the steak and top with 2 mushroom caps. Serve immediately.

SERVES 4

Béarnaise Sauce

The addition of 1 teaspoon tomato paste to this sauce will create a piquant and unusual Sauce Choron.

2 tablespoons finely chopped shallots
1 teaspoon crushed black peppercorns
1 tablespoon dried chervil
2 tablespoons dried tarragon

6 tablespoons red burgundy wine
3 tablespoons red wine vinegar
¹/₂ cup Hollandaise Sauce (see recipe on page 83-84)

1. Combine all of the ingredients, except the *Hollandaise Sauce,* in a saucepan and bring to a boil. Reduce heat and simmer until reduced to 2-4 tablespoons, about 15 minutes. Do not burn.

2. Mix 2 tablespoons of the reduction into the prepared *Hollandaise Sauce* and serve. Remainder of the reduction can be stored, covered, in the refrigerator for up to 3 months.

YIELD ¹/₂ CUP

John Wayne and Norman Rockwell.

COURTESY OF NORMAN ROCKWELL MUSEUM AT STOCKBRIDGE. PHOTO BY LOUIE LAMONE.

Welcome to The Red Lion Inn! Clockwise from left: fallen leaves, cornstocks, and pumpkins surround a Red Lion Inn sign in autumn; a stained glass window in Widow Bingham's Tavern; one of two lions that greet arriving guests.

When the air turns chilly, a fire is lighted in The Red Lion Inn's cozy lobby.

This whimsical folk art painting of the inn by Regi Klein hangs in the Dining Room.

The Roasted Sugar Beet & Goat Cheese Terrine is as colorful as it is delicious.

The Red Lion's gift shop, the Pink Kitty, is a fantasyland year-round, but especially at Christmas.

The Baked Onion Soup is rich and hearty. It's photographed here in a terrine with lion's head handles, although it will generally be presented in traditional brown crocks.

When the nearby fields hold stalks of fresh corn, the Red Lion Inn chef creates this tasty Roasted Corn Chowder for inn guests.

Roasted Loin of Pork.

This display is only part of the extensive collection of Colonial china that is found throughout the inn.

The charming McGregor House was restored by the Fitzpatricks and now contains two guest suites. It is located just behind the Red Lion Inn. Opposite and this page: views of the Dorothy and Bessie suite, which is on the second floor; bottom opposite: a view of the pretty side porch.

A Paillard of Chicken with Apple & Escarole Ragout sits in a pool of Dijon Vinaigrette.

Grilled Salmon Fillet with Lentils.

Giant pumpkins and cornstalks greet Red Lion Inn guests in autumn.

The Main Dining Room of The Red Lion Inn is set up for lunch in this photograph. It becomes a romantic, candlelit enchantress at night.

Red Lion Inn Whipped Butternut Squash

The original fire house in Stockbridge was built in 1898. It now contains a charming and handsome suite.

Red Lion Inn Apple Pie with Vanilla Ice Cream – a perennial favorite.

Apple-Cranberry Crisp.

Veal Oscar

The exact origin of Veal Oscar is in dispute, but it was first known as Kalvfilet Oskar. Authors Mary and Vincent Price, in their anthology of recipes from their favorite 1940s restaurants titled *A Treasury of Great Recipes,* say: "There are all kinds of romantic stories about who invented this dish, with credit going sometimes to Sweden's King Oskar, sometimes to Oscar of the Waldorf, and sometimes to any chef or maître d'hôtel who is telling it — especially if his name is Oskar or Oscar." Regardless, The Red Lion Inn's version of veal cutlets with asparagus spears and lobster, instead of the traditional crabmeat, offers a fabulous and unique rendition on this time-honored favorite.

12 asparagus spears
4 veal cutlets, pounded very thin (6-8 ounces each)
flour
salt and black pepper
2 tablespoons butter
1 cup cooked lobster meat
Hollandaise Sauce (see recipe below)

1. Steam the asparagus in a vegetable steamer until tender-crisp, about 5 minutes. Set aside.

2. Dredge the veal in the flour, seasoned with the salt and black pepper.

3. Melt the butter in a skillet. Add the cutlets and sauté over medium-high heat for 2 minutes on each side. Transfer the cutlets to a serving platter or individual plates.

4. Place a portion of the lobster meat on top of each piece of veal and top each serving with 3 asparagus spears. Spoon the prepared *Hollandaise Sauce* over the top and serve immediately.

SERVES 4

Hollandaise Sauce
4 egg yolks
4 1/2 tablespoons fresh lemon juice
2 tablespoons cold water

1 cup clarified butter, melted (see page 44)
salt and cayenne pepper to taste
¹/₄ teaspoon Worcestershire sauce

1. Place the egg yolks, lemon juice, and water in a double boiler over boiling water. Cook, whisking with a wire whisk, until the mixture has a light custard consistency, about 10-15 minutes. Remove from heat and whip until the custard falls slightly, about 1 minute.

2. Slowly whisk in the butter, a little at a time. Season with the salt, cayenne pepper, and Worcestershire sauce. Use immediately. This sauce will keep in the refrigerator for 2-3 days.

YIELD 1 ¹/₂ CUPS

The Country Curtains shop at The Red Lion Inn.

Veal Piccata

4 veal cutlets (6-8 ounces each)
$^1/_2$ cup flour
$^1/_2$ cup butter
$^1/_2$ cup white wine
2 tablespoons fresh lemon juice
$^1/_4$ cup capers
$^1/_2$ cup cold butter
4 teaspoons chopped fresh parsley

1. Pound the cutlets until thin and dredge in the flour.

2. Melt the butter in a sauté pan. Add the cutlets and sauté over medium-high heat for 2 minutes on each side. Transfer the cutlets to a platter and keep warm.

3. Add the wine, lemon juice, and capers to the sauté pan and boil until reduced to a syrup, about 5 minutes.

4. Remove from heat and add the butter. Gently melt the butter by shaking the pan so the sauce does not separate. Pour the sauce over the cutlets and sprinkle with the parsley. Serve immediately.

SERVES 4

Calves Liver with Bacon & Onions

¹/₂ cup flour
salt and black pepper
1 ¹/₂ - 2 pounds calves liver (8 pieces)
³/₄ cup vegetable oil or bacon drippings
2 small onions, thinly sliced
8 strips bacon, cooked

1. Season the flour with the salt and black pepper and dredge the liver in the flour, shaking off excess.

2. Heat the oil in a sauté pan. Add the liver and sauté over medium-high heat for 5 minutes on one side and 4 minutes on the other side. Transfer the liver to a heated platter and keep warm.

3. Reduce heat to medium and add the onions to the pan. Adjust the seasonings and cook until tender, about 5 minutes. Arrange the onions over the liver and top with the bacon strips. Serve immediately.

SERVES 4

Roasted Loin of Pork

You should begin preparing this dish on the day before you plan to serve it.

2 tablespoons herbs du Provence
1 teaspoon ground coriander
1 teaspoon kosher salt
2 ¹/₂ - 3 pounds tenderloin of pork, trimmed, rolled, and tied
1 cup packed brown sugar

1. Combine the herbs du Provence, coriander, and salt in a small bowl. Rub the pork loin throughly with the mixture.

2. Place the pork loin on a square of plastic wrap and coat with the brown sugar. Wrap the loin in the plastic wrap and refrigerate for at least 24 hours.

3. Preheat oven to 350° F.

4. Remove the loin from the plastic wrap and wipe the brown sugar from the outside of the loin and discard. Do not rinse the loin. Insert a meat thermometer in the center and place on a rack in a roasting pan. Roast until the thermometer registers 185°, about 40-45 minutes, or until the juices run clear and the meat is slightly gray.

5. Remove from oven and let stand for 10 minutes before slicing. Cut the loin into half inch slices and serve, if desired, with applesauce or mashed potatoes.

SERVES 6

"For all is good in thee;
Thy flesh, thy lard, thy muscles and thy tripe!
As galatine thou'rt loved, as blood pudding adored.
A saint has, of thy feet, created the best type
Of trotters. And, from the Périgord,
The soil has blessed thee with so sweet a scent
It could have woo'd Xantippe, all her anger spent
To join with Socrates, whom elsewise she abhorred
In worship of this lord
Of animals, dear hog: angelic meat, say we."

— Charles Monselet, a nineteenth-century
gastronomic writer, waxed poetic about the pig

Braised Lamb Shanks with Shaker-Style Mustard Butter

2 tablespoons olive oil
6 lamb shanks, including bone (about 5-6 pounds)
2 ¹/₂ medium onions, chopped
1 carrot, chopped
5 stalks celery, chopped
¹/₄ cup minced garlic
1 cup chopped fresh mushrooms
1 cup chopped tomatoes
2 whole juniper berries
3 bay leaves
4 sprigs fresh thyme, rinsed
¹/₂ cup plus 2 tablespoons Madeira wine
2 cups veal stock
2 cups beef or lamb stock
2 cups water
Shaker-Style Mustard Butter (see recipe below)

1. Heat the oil in a large pot. Add the shanks and brown on all sides. Remove the shanks and set aside.

2. Add the onions, carrot, celery, and garlic to the pot and sauté over low heat until the onions are translucent. Increase the heat slightly and continue to cook, stirring frequently, until the vegetables are caramelized. Do not burn.

3. Reduce heat to simmer. Add the mushrooms, tomatoes, juniper berries, bay leaves, and thyme and sauté until the vegetables are soft, about 20 minutes.

4. Add the wine and briskly stir with a wooden spoon to deglaze, scraping the bottom to loosen all particles.

5. Return the reserved shanks to the pot. Add both stocks and the water and simmer over low heat until the meat is tender and comes off the bone easily, about 2 hours.

6. Place 1 shank, including bone, in each of 6 pasta bowls and pour a bit of cooking sauce over each. Top with a dollop of the prepared *Shaker-Style Mustard Butter*.

SERVES 6

Shaker-Style Mustard Butter

Besides using this butter with *Braised Lamb Shanks,* you might pipe a rosette of this tangy butter on top of grilled steaks.

2 bunches fresh chives
1 tablespoon olive oil
1 cup whipped butter, at room temperature
$1/_2$ cup Dijon mustard
$1/_4$ cup chopped fresh rosemary
$1/_4$ cup chopped fresh parsley
salt and black pepper to taste

1. Place the bunches of chives and the oil in a blender and blend on medium speed until smooth.

2. Place the butter in a bowl and blend in $1/_8$ cup of the chive mixture, the mustard, rosemary, and parsley. Add the salt and black pepper. The butter can be stored, covered, in the refrigerator for up to 2 weeks.

3. When ready to use, allow to soften slightly, then place some of the butter in a pastry bag fitted with a rosette tip and pipe onto meat.

YIELD 1 $1/_2$ CUPS

Roast Long Island Duckling with Cranberry Glaze

White Pekin ducks, with more succulent meat than domestic ducks, were imported from China to the East End of Long Island in the 1870s. By 1939, there were ninety duck farms in the tiny village of Quogue alone, and by 1969, Suffolk County was raising sixty percent of the nation's ducks. William Stevens, in his 1939 book *Discovering Long Island,* accurately described a mounting problem, however. "But he (the duck) is something of a whited sepulcher, for all his angelic plumage. Each little White Pekin is a most active fertilizer factory, and when the wind is right, not all the perfumes of Araby could sweeten this little land of duck farms." Since that time, due to increasing land values, environmental (soil pollution) problems, and objections to the smell, the production has diminished to about fifteen percent of the national consumption. Nevertheless, Long Island ducks are still the aristocrat of the genre and are still used at The Red Lion Inn.

1 Long Island duckling (5 $^1/_2$ - 6 pounds)
$^1/_2$ apple, peeled, cored, and diced
1 small onion, diced
$^1/_8$ lemon, peeled and diced
$^1/_4$ orange, peeled, sectioned, and diced
2 bay leaves
salt and black pepper
2 tablespoons honey
3 tablespoons soy sauce
pinch ground ginger
Cranberry Demi-Glace (see recipe below)

1. Preheat oven to 325° F. Spray the rack of a roasting pan with cooking spray.
2. Remove the neck and giblets from the duck and trim off excess skin and fat. Thoroughly rinse out the cavity and pat dry. Combine the apple, onion, lemon, orange, and bay leaves in a bowl and place the mixture in the duck cavity. Prick the top and sides of the duck with a fork (this allows the fat to drain, while the duck is roasting). Season the skin with the salt and black pepper.

3. Place the duck in the prepared pan and roast for 3 hours. Remove from oven and drain off all fat, reserving the fat for the *Duck Espagnole* (see recipe below). Allow the duck to rest while preparing the *Duck Espagnole* and *Cranberry Demi-Glace.*

4. Preheat oven to 250° F. Mix together the honey, soy sauce, and ginger in a small bowl. Cook the duck for 10 minutes more, basting with the honey mixture twice. Serve with the prepared *Cranberry Demi-Glace.*

SERVES 4

Duck Espagnole

¹/₄ cup duck fat (see above)
¹/₂ medium onion, chopped
1 carrot, chopped
2 stalks celery, chopped
1 clove garlic, diced
2 shallots, chopped
1 medium tomato, chopped
2 tablespoons tomato paste
2 bay leaves
1 teaspoon dried thyme
1 teaspoon black pepper
1 teaspoon dried rosemary
2 quarts duck stock
1 cup butter
1 cup flour
salt to taste

1. Heat the fat in a large pot. Add the onion, carrot, celery, garlic, shallots, and tomato and sauté over low heat until the vegetables are light brown and tender, about 30 minutes.

2. Add the tomato paste, bay leaves, thyme, black pepper, and rosemary and cook for 10 minutes more. Add the stock and simmer for 2 hours.

3. Melt the butter in a small saucepan. Stir in the flour and blend thoroughly to make a roux. Cook over medium heat, stirring constantly, for 2-3 minutes.

4. Add the roux to the stock and cook until the sauce is thickened and reduced to 1 quart, about 1 hour.

5. Skim off fat, strain, and add the salt.

YIELD 4 CUPS

Cranberry Demi-Glace

¹/₄ cup sugar
1 tablespoon fresh lemon juice
2 tablespoons fresh orange juice
6 tablespoons cranberry juice
1 tablespoon currant jelly
¹/₄ cup Cointreau liqueur
4 cups Duck Espagnole (see recipe above)
1 bag fresh cranberries (12 ounces)

1. Cook the sugar in a large saucepan over medium heat, stirring constantly, until it melts and turns a light brown color, about 5-6 minutes. Do not burn. Remove the saucepan from the heat.

2. Slowly add the remaining ingredients, except the cranberries, to the caramelized sugar. The sugar will harden, but stir the mixture together thoroughly and return to the heat. As the ingredients warm, the caramel mixture will soften. Cook over medium heat, stirring occasionally, until reduced by one-third, about 40 minutes.

3. Stir in the cranberries and boil until the cranberries pop, about 5-6 minutes.

YIELD 2 ¹/₂ - 3 CUPS

"Will Hawkins used to shoot quail and partridge during open season for The Red Lion Inn table...."

— *The Springfield Union,* September 12, 1943

Sirloin of Venison with Red Wine Sauce

This hearty, peppery dish is a favorite of guests at The Red Lion Inn, especially in the late fall.

³/₄ cup butter
1 ¹/₂ pounds venison, cut into steaks or medallions ¹/₄" - ¹/₂" thick
¹/₂ cup flour
³/₄ cup sliced fresh shiitake mushroom caps
³/₄ cup sliced fresh oyster mushroom caps
2 teaspoons whole black peppercorns
4 tablespoons minced shallots
2 teaspoons dried thyme
¹/₄ cup red wine
¹/₄ cup Glace de Viande (see recipe below)

1. Melt ¹/₂ cup of the butter in a sauté pan. Dredge the venison in the flour and sauté over medium heat, turning once, until cooked to taste (rare is best, 6-8 minutes). Remove the venison from the pan and keep warm.

2. Add all of the mushrooms to the same sauté pan and cook until the mushroom liquid has evaporated, about 5 minutes.

3. Meanwhile, crack the peppercorns by placing on a cutting surface and pressing firmly with the bottom of a heavy skillet. Add the cracked pepper, shallots, thyme, and wine to the mushrooms and cook over high heat until reduced by half, about 3 minutes.

4. Add the prepared *Glace de Viande,* and swirl in the remaining ¹/₄ cup butter. Heat, but do not allow to boil or will separate. Place the reserved venison on a serving platter and pour the sauce over the top. Serve immediately.

SERVES 4

Glace de Viande

Glace de Viande is a syrupy, strong-flavored derivative of a basic stock. It can be made from beef, chicken, or veal stock. A small amount will add a rich flavor to any dish.

2 cups beef stock

1. Place the stock in a saucepan over high heat and bring to a boil. Reduce to simmer and cook (skimming any fat from surface) until reduced to a very thick, dark consistency, about 5-6 hours.

2. Use immediately or allow to cool (will have a rubbery quality). This glace can be stored in a tightly covered container in the refrigerator until ready to use and will keep for up to 3 months.

YIELD $1/4$ CUP

This fanciful drawing of The Red Lion was penned by author and illustrator Jan Brett, who came to the inn in December 1998 to autograph copies of Clement Moore's The Night Before Christmas, *which she illustrated with charming scenes featuring The Red Lion Inn in the background.*

CHAPTER 8

Seafood & Poultry

The abundance of cod and its early popularity are often emphasized when discussing New England food. This profusion is partly explained by Mrs. Isabella Beeton in her 1861 book *Beeton's Book of Household Management:* "So extensive has been the consumption of this fish, that it is surprising that it has not long ago become extinct. . . . Yet it ceases to excite our wonder when we remember that the female can every year give birth to more than 9,000,000 [eggs] at a time."

Benjamin Franklin, who considered himself a confirmed vegetarian, could nevertheless be lured into eating cod it appears, by this excerpt from his notes: "Being becalmed off Block Island, our people set about catching cod, and hauled up a great many. Hitherto I had stuck to my resolution of not eating animal food, and on this occasion I considered . . . the taking of every fish as a kind of unprovoked murder. . . . But I had formerly been a great lover of fish, and, when this came hot out of the frying-pan, it smelt admirably well. I balanced some time between principle and inclination, till I recollected that, when the fish were opened, I saw smaller fish taken out of their stomachs; then thought I, 'If you eat one another, I don't see why we mayn't eat you.' So I dined upon cod very heartily. . . . So convenient a thing it is to be a reasonable creature, since it enables one to find or make a reason for every thing one has a mind to do."

The abundance of salmon, especially in early summer, led to yet another New England tradition. Eastern salmon begin to "run" about the Fourth of July of each year, just as new vegetables are popping up in the garden. To celebrate, poached salmon with egg sauce, along with the first new potatoes and early peas, have become the traditional Fourth of July fare.

Oysters were in abundance, too — to such an extent in the early days that they were dumped into soups by the hundreds.

By the mid-1800s, the country was in the midst of an oyster craze. They were eaten raw, baked, fried, fricasseed, used in soups, pies, stuffings, and perched atop steaks.

Coastal cities in Massachusetts boasted specialized oyster houses where the signs offered "All you can eat" for five or six cents.

A drawing of Jack and Jane Fitzpatrick by illustrator Al Hirschfeld, rendered as part of the festivities surrounding the seventieth anniversary gala of the Berkshire Theatre Festival in 1998. Can you find the three places where the artist included his daughter Nina's name?

Grilled Salmon Fillets with Lentils

2 tablespoons olive oil
1 medium white onion, minced
1 carrot, minced
2 stalks celery, minced
1 ham hock, cut into 2 pieces
4 cups apple juice
4 cups chicken stock
1 bay leaf
6 black peppercorns
1 pound French green lentils
$^1/_2$ pound fresh spinach, washed
salt and black pepper
3 pounds fresh salmon, cut into 6 fillets

1. Heat 1 tablespoon of the oil in a large pot and sauté $^1/_2$ cup of the onions, the carrot, celery, and ham hock until the vegetables are soft and the onions are translucent, about 5-7 minutes. Add 2 cups of the apple juice, 2 cups of the stock, the bay leaf, and peppercorns. Bring to a boil and reduce by half. Set aside.

2. Heat the remaining oil in another pot and sauté the remaining onions until translucent, about 5-7 minutes. Add the lentils and sauté over medium heat for 3 minutes more. Add the remaining apple juice and stock and simmer over medium heat until the lentils are soft, but not mushy. Set aside.

3. Place the spinach in a pot of boiling, salted water and blanch for 2-3 minutes. Season with the salt and black pepper. Remove the spinach from the water and drain well.

4. Lightly sprinkle more salt and black pepper on both sides of the fillets. Grill the salmon until lightly browned on both sides, but still pink and moist in the center.

5. To serve, pile several spinach leaves in the center of each of 6 wide-rimmed soup bowls and spoon one-sixth of the lentils around the spinach. Lay a fillet on top of the spinach and lentils and spoon the reserved broth over the top.

SERVES 6

Poached Fillet of Salmon

Although traditionally, this dish is served on the Fourth of July as new vegetables are beginning to appear, it is a lovely dish served year-round, especially with this sauce — just as it's served at The Red Lion Inn.

1 stalk celery, chopped
6 sprigs fresh parsley, rinsed and chopped
1 leek, chopped (white part only)
2 bay leaves
12 black peppercorns
4 cups fish stock or water
3 cups white wine
$^1/_4$ cup pickling spices
2 lemons, quartered
4 fillets of salmon (8 ounces each)
chopped fresh dill (optional)
1 cup Hollandaise Sauce (see recipe on pages 83-84)

1. Prepare a bouquet garni by placing the celery, parsley, leek, bay leaves, and peppercorns on a 6" square of cheesecloth. Tie up to form a small bag.

2. Combine the stock, wine, pickling spices, lemon quarters, and bouquet garni in a large pot and bring to a boil. Reduce heat and simmer for 15 minutes.

3. Add the fillets to the broth and poach over low heat until the fish flakes when gently prodded with a fork, about 15-20 minutes.

4. Stir the dill into the prepared *Hollandaise Sauce*.

5. Remove the fillets from the broth and arrange on a warm serving platter. Top with the sauce and serve immediately.

SERVES 4

Fillet of Sole Veronique

This is an elegant and unusual presentation of that tasty New England flatfish, the sole.

2 tablespoons butter
3 tablespoons flour
2 cups fish stock
2 ¹/₂ pounds fillet of sole
4 cups white wine
²/₃ cup Hollandaise Sauce (see recipe on pages 83-84)
²/₃ cup cream, whipped
salt and black pepper
1 bunch seedless green grapes (about 30)

1. Preheat oven to 325° F. Grease a baking dish, large enough to place the sole in a single layer.

2. Melt the butter in a sauté pan. Add the flour and cook over medium heat until blended, about 2-3 minutes. Add 1 cup of the fish stock and cook over low heat until reduced to ¹/₂ cup, about 30-45 minutes. Allow to cool.

3. Roll up the fillets and place in the prepared dish, seam side down. Cover completely with the remaining stock and the white wine and bake until the fish flakes when gently prodded with a fork, about 8-10 minutes. Remove the dish from the oven and allow the fish to cool in the broth, about 15 minutes.

4. Preheat broiler. Combine the prepared *Hollandaise Sauce* and the whipped cream, folding lightly together. Fold the mixture into the cooled fish stock. Drain the poached fish, reserving the stock, and arrange on a flameproof platter.

5. Sprinkle the fish with the salt and black pepper. Scatter the grapes over the fish and pour the sauce over all. Broil until delicately browned, about 3-5 minutes. Serve immediately.

SERVES 6

Grilled Marinated Tuna

2 cups soy sauce
*$^1/_4$ cup chili-garlic sauce**
$^1/_2$ cup Dijon mustard
Four 6- to 8-ounce fresh tuna steaks, or one 2-pound fresh tuna loin, cut into 4 steaks

1. Whisk together both sauces and the mustard in a bowl. Pour the mixture into a container deep enough to hold the steaks.

2. Place the steaks in the marinade and turn once to coat. Cover and refrigerate for 3-12 hours, occasionally turning the steaks.

3. Grill the steaks over medium heat until rare to medium rare, tender but juicy. Do not overcook, as tuna tends to dry out quickly.

SERVES 4

* Available in Asian markets or large supermarkets.

> "(If) you like your dinner, man; never be ashamed to say so. . . remember that every man who has been worth a fig in this world, as poet, painter, or musician, has had a good appetite and a good taste."
>
> — William Makepeace Thackeray, *Memorials of Gormandizing*, 1852

Pan-Seared Sea Bass with Barley Purse & Ginger-Carrot Broth

Barley Purses:
1 tablespoon olive oil
1 medium white onion, minced
2 cups uncooked pearl barley
12 cups chicken stock
12 fresh leaves Swiss chard

Ginger-Carrot Broth:
1 large piece fresh gingerroot, peeled
2 cups carrot juice
salt and black pepper to taste
1 tablespoon butter

Sea Bass:
3 tablespoons olive oil
2 pounds fresh sea bass, cut into 4 fillets
salt and black pepper

1. For the barley purses: (can be prepared one day ahead) Heat the oil in a large pot and sauté the onion until translucent, about 2-3 minutes.

2. Mix in the barley until well coated with oil. Add the stock and bring to a boil. Immediately reduce heat to simmer and continue to cook, stirring frequently, until the barley is just cooked (soft, but not mushy). Spread the mixture on an ungreased baking sheet and allow to cool in the refrigerator.

3. Prepare a bowl of ice water. Drop the chard leaves in a pot of salted, boiling water and boil until blanched, about 2 minutes. Remove the chard from the water and immerse the leaves in the prepared ice water.

4. Grease four 3" wide x 2" tall ring molds (cookie or biscuit cutters can be used). Take 3 cooled chard leaves and line the inside of the mold, allowing excess to hang over the sides. Gently pack the mold with the barley mixture and fold the chard leaves over the barley to cover. Repeat for the remaining three molds. Remove the barley "purses" from the molds and wrap in plastic wrap. Refrigerate until ready to use.

5. When ready to use, remove the "purses" from the refrigerator and place in a bamboo steamer over a pot of boiling water. Steam for 12-15 minutes.

6. For the ginger-carrot broth: Place the gingerroot in a juicer to extract juice. Combine $1/_4$ cup of the ginger juice and the carrot juice in a saucepan and bring to a boil over medium heat. Reduce heat to simmer and cook gently for 10 minutes. Add the salt and black pepper. Just before serving, whisk in the butter.

7. For the sea bass: Drizzle 1 tablespoon of the oil over the fillets and season with the salt and black pepper.

8. Heat the remaining oil in a sauté pan until almost smoking. Add the fillets and sauté on one side until the fillets are golden brown and crisp, about 3-4 minutes. Turn the fillets and sauté until crisp and flaky, but still moist.

9. To serve: Place a barley purse into each of 4 wide-rimmed soup bowls. Lean a fillet against each "purse" and spoon the ginger-carrot broth around the sides. Serve.

SERVES 4

"Who'er has traveled life's dull round,
Where'er his stages may have been,
May sigh to think he has yet found
His warmest welcome at an inn
                                        — Old Tavern Song

Baked Boston Scrod

4 fillets of scrod (6-8 ounces each)
salt and black pepper
2 tablespoons fresh lemon juice
1 $1/_2$ cups white wine
$1/_2$ cup butter, melted
1 cup dried bread crumbs

1. Preheat oven to 350° F. Grease a baking dish, large enough to place the scrod in a single layer.

2. Place the fillets in the prepared dish and add the salt, black pepper, lemon juice, and wine. Drizzle $1/_4$ cup of the butter over the fish and bake until the fish flakes but is still moist, about 20 minutes.

3. Remove the dish from the oven and preheat broiler.

4. Scatter the bread crumbs over the fillets and drizzle the remaining butter over the top. Brown under the broiler until lightly browned, about 2-5 minutes only. Serve immediately.

SERVES 4

According to Hilde Gabriel Lee in Taste of the States: A Food History of America, *there is no such fish as a scrod. She says, "Contrary to what fish markets and restaurants would have us believe, there is no such fish as scrod. The name "scrod" was invented in the nineteenth century by the maître d'hôtel of the Parker House in Boston to assure his clientele that they were eating the freshest fish possible.*

"At that time, fishing vessels spent up to ten days at the Great Banks off the coasts of Maine and Massachusetts. The first day's catch was gutted and iced down in the bottom of the boat. Subsequent days' catches were put on top until the vessel was full. The ship then sped to the Boston Fish Pier, where the catch was auctioned.

"The Parker House chef insisted on buying only the freshest fish from the top layer. Since the maître d'hôtel had to get his menus printed a day in advance, and since he could not predict what fish would be on top, he coined the word "scrod." Today, scrod has come to mean a small fish of the cod family — cod, haddock, hake, or pollock — weighing one and a half to two and a half pounds.

Caramelized Sea Scallops with Peanuts & Bok Choy

4 cups fresh orange juice
1 cup shelled peanuts
1 cup corn oil
1 tablespoon smooth peanut butter
3 tablespoons corn oil
1 teaspoon peeled and minced fresh gingerroot
¹⁄₂ shallot, minced
1 clove garlic, minced
¹⁄₄ cup soy sauce
1 cup chicken stock
1¹⁄₂ - 2 pounds fresh sea scallops
salt and black pepper
1 carrot, halved and cut diagonally into ¹⁄₈" thick pieces
1 head baby bok choy, washed, end trimmed, and head quartered
4 fresh asparagus tips, cut into 2 ¹⁄₂" pieces
3 ounces trimmed fresh snow peas (about 15-20)
1 leek, julienned
1 teaspoon butter

1. Place the orange juice in a large saucepan and bring to a boil. Continue to boil, stirring frequently, until mixture is consistency of light syrup (should have at least 1 cup). Allow to cool.

2. Roast the peanuts in a sauté pan until lightly browned. Add just enough of the 1 cup corn oil to reach two-thirds to the top of the peanuts and sauté the roasted peanuts for 2-3 minutes. Drain the oil from the peanuts (reserving the oil) and grind the peanuts in a food processor until chunky. Add a bit of the roasting oil, if needed, to assist with the grinding.

3. Combine the ground peanuts, the smooth peanut butter, and 1 cup of the cooled orange juice syrup in a bowl and mix together with a spoon. Set aside.

4. Heat 1 tablespoon of the corn oil in a saucepan and sauté the gingerroot, shallot, and garlic until translucent, about 4-5 minutes. Add the soy sauce and bring to a boil. Add

the stock and return to a boil. Simmer for about 15 minutes. Strain the broth mixture and set aside.

5. Heat the remaining 2 tablespoons corn oil in a sauté pan over high heat until almost smoking. Sprinkle the scallops with the salt and black pepper and place in the hot corn oil. Stir rapidly, searing the scallops until golden brown on all sides, about 2-3 minutes per side. Remove the scallops from the pan and keep warm.

6. Add the carrot to the sauté pan and sauté about 3 minutes. Add the bok choy, asparagus, snow peas, and leek and sauté for 3 minutes more. Add the reserved broth mixture and bring to a boil. Reduce heat, add the butter, and mix in well. Adjust the seasonings.

7. To serve, place one-fourth of the broth mixture in the bottom of each of 4 wide-rimmed soup bowls. Top each bowl with one-fourth of the scallops. Garnish each serving with one-fourth of the reserved peanut-orange mixture.

SERVES 4

The cod was so important to Massachusetts economically that on March 17, 1784, the House of Representatives of the Commonwealth of Massachusetts voted to hang a representation of a cod in their chamber. Although it's been moved to new quarters several times since, it continues to hang in the current House chambers, as a perpetual reminder of the importance of the cod to the early welfare of the Commonwealth.

Shrimp Scampi

16 fresh jumbo shrimp
16 fresh clams
1 pound cooked angel hair or fettuccine pasta
4 teaspoons olive oil
1 cup butter
2 tablespoons minced garlic
1 cup white wine
2 teaspoons dried oregano
2 teaspoons dried basil
pinch cayenne pepper

1. Peel the shrimp, leaving the tail section on. Split the shrimp along the back from tail to head, but do not slice through. Remove the vein and rinse thoroughly.

2. Wash the clams thoroughly.

3. Cook the pasta in a pot of boiling, salted water for 6-7 minutes if using angel hair, for 8-10 minutes if using fettuccine. Drain the pasta and toss with the oil in a large bowl. Keep warm.

4. Melt the butter in a large sauté pan. Lightly sauté the garlic over low-medium heat until soft and transparent. Stir in the shrimp, clams, wine, herbs, and cayenne pepper. Cook until the shrimp are pink and the clams have opened, about 6-7 minutes. Discard any clams that do not open.

5. Serve the shrimp and clams over the hot pasta.

SERVES 4

In 1622, when a group of new colonists arrived in Plymouth, Governor William Bradford was deeply humiliated because his colony was so short of food that the only "dish they could presente their friends with was a lobster. . . without bread or anything els but a cupp of fair water."

Chicken Breast Almandine

¹/₂ cup flour
salt and black pepper
¹/₂ cup milk
2 eggs
1 cup dried bread crumbs
1 cup sliced blanched almonds (see page 26)
2 whole chicken breasts, boned, skinned, and split into 4 pieces
¹/₄ cup vegetable oil
¹/₂ cup butter
1 cup Hollandaise Sauce (see recipe on pages 83-84)

1. Preheat oven to 375° F. Grease a baking pan large enough to hold the chicken in a single layer.

2. Mix together the flour, salt, and black pepper in a shallow dish. Beat together the milk and eggs in another shallow dish. Combine the bread crumbs and ¹/₂ cup of the almonds in a third dish. Dip each chicken piece first in the flour mixture, then in the egg mixture, and then in the bread crumb mixture.

3. Heat the oil and ¹/₄ cup of the butter in a heavy skillet and sauté the chicken over medium heat until golden brown, about 3-4 minutes on each side. Transfer the chicken to the prepared pan and bake for 10-15 minutes.

4. Melt the remaining butter in a sauté pan and sauté the remaining almonds over low heat until lightly browned, about 5 minutes.

5. Top the chicken with the prepared *Hollandaise Sauce* and garnish with the sautéed almonds. Serve.

SERVES 4

Paillard of Chicken with Apple & Escarole Ragout

3 tablespoons olive oil
1 large white onion, julienned
2 Macoun apples, unpeeled and sliced
3 cups rinsed and chopped fresh escarole
2 cups apple cider
4 whole boneless chicken breasts, split and lightly pounded
salt and black pepper
Dijon Vinaigrette (see recipe below)

1. Heat 2 tablespoons of the oil in a sauté pan and sauté the onion until caramelized. Add the apple slices, escarole, and cider and cook on high heat until the escarole is wilted and the cider is almost evaporated.

2. Lightly season the chicken with the salt and black pepper. In another pan, heat the remaining oil and sauté the chicken over medium heat for about 3 minutes on each side. Do not overcook.

3. To assemble, pour one-fourth of the prepared *Dijon Vinaigrette* on 4 individual plates and place $^1/_2$ cup of the apple/escarole ragout in the center of each plate. Arrange a chicken breast on the mixture and top each with $^1/_4$ cup ragout. Serve.

SERVES 4

Dijon Vinaigrette

$^1/_2$ *cup whole grain Dijon mustard*
$^1/_4$ *cup olive oil*
$^1/_4$ *cup cider vinegar*

Whisk all of the ingredients together in a small bowl until thoroughly blended.

YIELD 1 CUP

CHAPTER 9

Vegetables, Rice & Potatoes

Early New Englanders lived off the bounty of the land and grew an abundance of vegetables, fruit, berries, and grains. Fresh vegetables were always preferred, but when the supply was overly abundant, vegetables were stewed or made into a sauce, which frugal Pilgrim housewives called garden sass. These sauces were then poured over meat and fish to give them variety.

From the surviving letters of John and Abigail Adams, we learn about the trials of early farm life in Massachusetts. Abigail was often left with the duties of running the farm, while John attended to his duties as vice president or president of the new United States. Yet it was John who always voiced a preference for "the Delights of a Garden to the Dominion of a World." Even after moving to Washington, D.C., Abigail made sure that John was regularly provided with "fresh russet potatoes" and the "sweet apples from our tree."

Waverly Root says in *Food* that the green bean or *haricot* was not only an important food of the Indians in the cold, damp Northeast, but also one of two chief ingredients in their succotash (the other being Indian corn). He goes on to say: "The haricot is the most versatile of all beans. It comprises tall climbing plants and low bush types. There are beans meant to be eaten young, pods and all, and beans which, though also eaten entire, can be so consumed even in maturity. There are round beans, oval beans, fat beans, flat beans, long beans, and kidney-shaped beans. There are white beans, yellow beans, tan beans, green beans, pink beans, red beans, purple beans, black beans, and mottled beans." The beans that the early settlers most used, however, were those incorporated into baked beans.

As early as 1584, Jacques Cartier, an explorer who was nosing around the St. Lawrence, reported finding melons (or pumpkins) growing. These pumpkins, which seem to be unique to the New World, were a treat enjoyed by the Indians, who taught the colonists how to cook them. In fact, Waverly Root in *Food* says: "Despite some assertions that European varieties of squash existed and despite the caution that persists to this day among botanists, who describe these vegetables as of uncertain origin but probably American, I think we may make bold to assert that squashes and pumpkins are uniquely American and were completely unknown to the Old World before the time of Columbus."

Corn, squash, and beans are generally mentioned as the first New England vegetables, and they remain popular today. Corn was used in a variety of ways, but it was often thought ill-mannered to eat it directly from the cob, as the following note from *The American Heritage Cookbook* indicates: "Some people take the whole stem," Fredrika Bremer wrote about her visit to America in 1850, "and gnaw [the kernels] out with their teeth: two gentlemen do so who sit opposite... myself at table, and who we call 'the sharks.'"

Various owners of The Red Lion Inn often maintained a garden behind the inn from which they supplied their tables with fresh vegetables. According to an unsigned letter in The Red Lion Inn scrapbook, dated November 8, 1929, (when the Plumbs owned the inn), "The owners had a garden where early vegetables were grown and were then, as now, a great luxury to the city visitors."

Although there is currently no garden in back of the inn, the inn is a dedicated member of "Berkshire Grown," an organization of inns and restaurants who are committed to serving produce grown in Berkshire County. Milton Bass wrote in a 1973 *Berkshire Eagle* article that "Mrs. Fitzpatrick is still farm girl enough to be happiest with fresh rather than frozen or canned." This preference for "fresh" is reflected in the following recipes.

Note: See Chapter 13, Holiday Time at The Red Lion Inn, for the recipe *Candied Yams with Bourbon.*

"It is not elegant to gnaw Indian corn. The kernels should be scored with a knife, scraped off into the plate, and then eaten with a fork. Ladies should be particularly careful how they manage so ticklish a dainty, lest the exhibition rub off a little desirable romance."

— *Hints on Etiquette*, 1844

Sautéed Zucchini with Cherry Tomatoes & Basil

1 bunch fresh basil, rinsed well (about 24 whole leaves)
$^1/_4$ cup olive oil
2 cloves garlic, chopped
1 pound fresh zucchini, thinly sliced
24 cherry tomatoes, cut in half
salt and black pepper to taste
pinch cayenne pepper
$^1/_4$ cup grated Parmesan cheese (optional)

1. Save the best basil leaves (about half) for garnish. Chop the remaining leaves and set aside.

2. Heat the oil and garlic in a skillet or wok over low heat for 3 minutes. Do not brown. Add the zucchini and sauté, stirring frequently, for 2-3 minutes. Add the tomatoes and stir-fry for 2-3 minutes. Add the reserved basil, salt, black pepper, and cayenne pepper and cook for 2 minutes more. Adjust the seasonings.

3. Place the zucchini mixture on a platter and garnish with the whole basil leaves. Sprinkle with the cheese, if desired, and serve.

SERVES 6-8

"The cherry tomato is a marvelous invention, producing as it does a satisfactorily explosive squish when bitten."

— Miss Manners

Red Lion Inn Whipped Butternut Squash

3 pounds butternut squash, peeled, seeded, and coarsely chopped
$^1/_2$ cup butter
$^1/_4$ cup firmly packed light brown sugar
2 tablespoons pure maple syrup
1 teaspoon salt
$^1/_2$ teaspoon white pepper
$^1/_2$ teaspoon ground nutmeg
chopped fresh parsley, for garnish

1. Preheat oven to 350° F. Grease a 3-quart baking dish.

2. Boil the squash in salted water to cover until tender, about 20 minutes. Drain well. While still hot, combine the squash with the remaining ingredients, except the parsley, in a mixing bowl. Whip with an electric mixer until smooth. Adjust the seasonings.

3. Spoon the squash mixture into the prepared dish, cover, and bake until piping hot, about 15 minutes. Garnish with the parsley and serve.

SERVES 10-12

Creamed Onions

20 small white onions, peeled (about 3 pounds)
2 cups milk
¹/₄ cup butter
¹/₄ cup flour
1 small onion, studded with 3 whole cloves
1 bay leaf
¹/₈ teaspoon ground nutmeg
salt and black pepper to taste
dash ground mace
¹/₄ cup minced fresh chives

1. Boil the onions in salted water to cover until tender, about 30 minutes. Drain well.

2. Bring the milk to a boil in a small saucepan. Melt the butter in another saucepan, then add the flour and cook over low heat, stirring constantly, for 2 minutes. Do not brown. Whisk in the hot milk and continue whisking until the sauce is smooth. Add the cloved onion, bay leaf, nutmeg, salt, black pepper, and mace and simmer for 20 minutes. Strain.

3. Add the drained onions to the cream sauce and reheat. Adjust the seasonings and sprinkle with the chives. Serve.

SERVES 6

Red Lion Inn Wild & Brown Rice

¹/₂ cup butter
³/₄ cup chopped onions
1 ¹/₂ cups chopped celery
¹/₄ cup dried marjoram
2 tablespoons garlic powder
dash salt and black pepper
2 bay leaves
5 cups beef broth
1 cup uncooked brown rice
1 cup uncooked wild rice

1. Melt the butter in a deep saucepan. Add the vegetables and seasonings and sauté over medium heat until the vegetables are soft, about 5-7 minutes. Remove the bay leaves.

2. Add the broth and bring to a boil. Add both rices, stir, and cover. Reduce heat and cook over medium heat until the rice is tender and has absorbed the broth, about 50-60 minutes. Serve.

SERVES 8

Red Lion Inn Rice

$^1/_2$ cup butter
2 stalks celery, finely chopped
$^1/_2$ medium onion, finely chopped
$^1/_2$ pound fresh mushrooms, wiped clean and finely chopped
2 tablespoons garlic powder
2 teaspoons dried thyme
2 bay leaves
dash salt and black pepper
4 cups chicken broth
2 cups uncooked white rice

1. Melt the butter in a deep saucepan. Add the vegetables and seasonings and sauté over medium heat until the vegetables are soft, about 5-7 minutes. Remove the bay leaves.

2. Add the broth and bring to a boil. Stir in the rice and cover. Reduce heat and cook over medium heat until the rice is tender and has absorbed the broth, about 30-45 minutes. Serve.

SERVES 8

Red Lion Inn Rosemary & Garlic Potatoes

2 tablespoons olive oil
6 medium Yukon Gold potatoes, peeled and quartered
1 tablespoon minced garlic
1 sprig fresh rosemary, rinsed and chopped
salt and black pepper to taste

1. Preheat oven to 350° F.

2. Heat the oil in an ovenproof baking dish over medium heat. Add the potatoes, garlic, rosemary, salt, and black pepper and sauté, stirring frequently, until the potatoes are caramelized. Do not brown the garlic.

3. Roast the caramelized potatoes in the oven until the potatoes are golden brown and tender when pierced with a fork, about 30 minutes. Serve.

SERVES 4

"Nor do I say, that it is filthy to eat potatoes. I do not ridicule the using of them as sauce. What I laugh at is, the idea of the use of them. . . in lieu of wheat. . . . As food for cattle, sheep or hogs, this is the worst of all the green and root crops; but of this I have said enough before; and therefore, I now dismiss the Potato with the hope, that I shall never again have to write the word, or see the thing."

— William Cobbett, *A Year's Residence in the United States of America*, 1819

Red Lion Potatoes

6 cups water
2 pounds medium potatoes, peeled
8 tablespoons butter
6 ounces hickory-smoked ham, diced
1 cup minced onions
$^1/_3$ cup heated heavy cream
salt and black pepper to taste
$^1/_4$ cup grated Parmesan cheese

1. Preheat oven to 375° F. Grease an 8" square baking dish.

2. Bring the water to a boil, add the potatoes, and cook until tender, about 30-40 minutes. Drain, but keep hot.

3. Melt 4 tablespoons of the butter in a skillet and sauté the ham and onions over medium heat just until the onions are translucent, about 5 minutes. Drain and set aside the cooking liquid.

4. Place the potatoes, 3 tablespoons of the remaining butter, the hot cream, the reserved cooking liquid, the salt, black pepper, and $^1/_8$ cup of the cheese in a mixing bowl and whip with an electric mixer until smooth. Add the ham and onions and adjust the seasonings.

5. Place the potato mixture in the prepared dish, dot with the remaining butter, and sprinkle with the remaining cheese. Bake until bubbly hot and golden, about 20-25 minutes. Serve.

SERVES 6-8

"Potatoes will clean linen as well as soap."

— Mrs. Isabella Beeton, *Beeton's Book of Household Management*, 1861

Baked Stuffed Potatoes Red Lion

8 baking potatoes, washed
4 teaspoons vegetable oil
$^1/_2$ cup hot milk
$^1/_2$ cup plus 2 tablespoons butter
2 tablespoons sour cream
1 $^1/_4$ teaspoons salt
$^1/_4$ teaspoon black pepper
3 tablespoons dried chives
2 tablespoons Dijon mustard
$^1/_4$ cup grated Parmesan cheese
$^1/_4$ cup bacon bits
ground paprika

1. Preheat oven to 350° F.

2. Rub the skins of the potatoes with the oil. Prick each potato twice with a fork and bake for 1 hour.

3. Cut the tops off the potatoes while still very hot. Scoop out the potato pulp (be careful not to pierce the skin) and combine with the hot milk, 5 tablespoons of the butter, the sour cream, salt, black pepper, chives, and mustard in a bowl. Whip the mixture with an electric mixer until smooth.

4. Place the whipped potato mixture in a pastry bag fitted with a star tip and pipe the filling back into the potato shells. Sprinkle with the cheese, bacon bits, and paprika. Melt the remaining butter and drizzle over the potatoes. Bake until the tops are golden crisp, about 10 minutes. Serve.

SERVES 8

Chantilly Potatoes

6 cups water
2 pounds medium potatoes, peeled
$1/4$ cup butter
$1/2$ teaspoon salt
$1/3$ cup heated heavy cream
3 tablespoons sour cream
1 teaspoon onion powder
white pepper to taste
cayenne pepper to taste
$1/4$ cup minced fresh chives

1. Bring the water to a boil, add the potatoes, and cook until tender, about 30-40 minutes. Drain, but keep hot.

2. Place the potatoes in a mixing bowl and whip with an electric mixer on low speed. Add the butter, salt, hot cream and whip until smooth. Add the sour cream, onion powder, white pepper, cayenne pepper, and chives and whip until just blended. Adjust the seasonings and serve immediately.

SERVES 6-8

CHAPTER 10

Pies & Cakes

Americans love desserts, especially pies and cakes. Apple pie was such a staple of early American cooking that it was eaten for breakfast, lunch, dinner, and supper. It was made in a variety of ways — with fresh sliced apples, with applesauce, or with dried apples.

It is said that the first orchards in New England were planted by William Blaxton, a clergyman who owned, for a time, a farm on Beacon Hill in Boston. He moved to Rhode Island in 1635 and raised what is now called the Sweet Rhode Island Greening — the first variety of apple grown in the United States.

Those first apple pies probably were not the melt-in-your-mouth types that we love today, for a Dr. Acrelius wrote in 1758, "House-pie, in country places, is made of apples neither peeled nor freed from their cores, and its crust is not broken if a wagon wheel goes over it."

By 1851, however, American housewives had learned a thing or two, according to an

assessment of an immigrant living in Wisconsin, who wrote to friends in Norway: "Strawberries, raspberries, and blackberries thrive here. From these they make a wonderful dish combined with syrup and sugar, which is called pai. I can tell you that is something that glides easily down your throat; they also make the same sort of pai out of apples or finely ground meat, with syrup added, and that is really the most superb."

As much as early settlers loved pies, however, one pie apparently came into disfavor shortly after the settlers arrived. Mincemeat pie at Christmas had been popular in England long before there was an America.

Nevertheless, according to Hilde Gabriel Lee in *Taste of the States: A Food History of America*: ". . . they banned Christmas mincemeat pie. The pie was baked in a dish that had come to symbolize the Christ Child's manger, and the spices used in the pie had come to represent the gifts of the Wise Men. The Puritans considered these symbols to be sacrilegious and passed laws not only outlawing the pie, but also all Christmas celebrations. Years later, mincemeat pie staged a comeback in the common round pie plate."

It's a good thing that most households had a few chickens to produce eggs for the family, because they were used prodigiously. Amelia Simmons in her 1796 book *American Cookery* offers a cake recipe calling for twenty pounds of flour, fifteen pounds of sugar, ten pounds of butter, and four dozen eggs. Mrs. Chadwick in *Home Cookery* includes a cake recipe that calls for ninety eggs, plus the whites of nineteen more for the frosting. Although these were wedding cakes, an ordinary cake recipe might ask for the yolks of thirty-two eggs.

Chocolate cake holds a festive place in most American kitchens, too, and since chocolate was first imported by a New Englander, it's especially popular in this region. In 1765, Dr. James Baker of Dorchester, Massachusetts, financed the first chocolate mill in America. Baker imported the cocoa beans from the West Indies, and a new industry was born.

The Red Lion Inn is justifiably noted for its desserts, including apple pie and chocolate cake. Some of the recipes have been handed down from generation to generation, while others are relatively new to The Red Lion Inn repertoire.

Note: See Chapter 13, Holiday Time at The Red Lion Inn, for the recipes *Pumpkin Pie* and *Mincemeat Pie.*

"But I, when I undress me.
Each night, upon my knees
Will ask the Lord to bless me
With apple-pie and cheese."

— Eugene Field,
Apple-Pie and Cheese, 1889

Red Lion Inn Apple Pie

President Calvin Coolidge said that he never ate anything half as good as the pork apple pies that his stepmother made. One hopes that the President and Mrs. Coolidge tried *Red Lion Inn Apple Pie* on one of their visits. We bet that it's every bit as good as his mother's.

5 pounds McIntosh or Cortland apples, peeled, cored, and sliced
1 cup plus 1 tablespoon sugar
2 teaspoons ground cinnamon
Pie Crust for Two-Crust Pie, unbaked (see recipe below)
1 tablespoon butter
1 egg
1 tablespoon milk

1. Preheat oven to 375° F.
2. Place the apples in a large bowl. Combine 1 cup of the sugar and the cinnamon in a small bowl, then add to the apples. Toss until well mixed.
3. Fill the prepared pie crust with the apple mixture and dot with the butter. Fit the top crust over the filling and crimp the top and bottom edges together.
4. Whisk together the egg and milk. Brush the top crust with this egg wash and sprinkle with the remaining sugar. Pierce the top crust in several places with a sharp knife and bake for 50-60 minutes, or until the apples are tender when tested with a thin knife.

YIELD 1 PIE

Pie Crust for Two-Crust Pie

$^1/_2$ cup cold butter
$^1/_2$ cup vegetable shortening
2 $^1/_4$ cups flour
$^3/_4$ teaspoon salt
$^1/_2$ cup cold milk

1. Blend the butter and shortening together with a wooden spoon in a small bowl.
2. Sift together the flour and salt in a large bowl. Cut in the butter and shortening

mixture, using a pastry blender or two knives, until the mixture resembles cornmeal. Add the cold milk and blend until absorbed. (Or, if using a food processor, place the butter, shortening, flour, and salt in the bowl, fitted with a steel blade. Process until the mixture reaches the consistency of cornmeal. With the processor on, add the milk slowly through the funnel until the dough forms a ball.)

3. Divide the dough in half and roll each half into a ball. Wrap in plastic wrap and refrigerate until chilled, about 30 minutes.

4. Roll out each half of the chilled pie dough on a floured surface until it is slightly larger than the pie plate. Fit one half into the pie plate, place a filling inside, add the top crust, and flute the edges together.

YIELD 2 CRUSTS

"We may live without friends,
we may live without books,
but civilized man cannot live without cooks."
— Owen Meredith

Blackberry & Apple Pie

2 ¹/₂ pounds apples, peeled, cored, and sliced
2 cups fresh or frozen blackberries
1 cup sugar
1 ¹/₂ teaspoons ground cinnamon
¹/₂ teaspoon ground nutmeg
2 tablespoons flour
Pie Crust for Two-Crust Pie, unbaked (see recipe on pages 122-123)
1 tablespoon butter
1 egg yolk
1 tablespoon milk

1. Preheat oven to 375° F.
2. Mix together the apples and blackberries in a large bowl.
3. Blend together all of the dry ingredients, then gently mix into the fruit. Spoon the filling into the prepared pie crust and dot with the butter. Fit the top crust over the filling and crimp the top and bottom edges together.
4. Whisk together the egg yolk and milk and brush the top crust with this egg wash. Pierce the top crust in several places with a sharp knife and bake for 1 hour 15 minutes, or until the apples are tender when poked with a thin knife. (If crust seems to be browning too quickly, reduce temperature to 325°.)

YIELD 1 PIE

Pecan Pie

²/₃ cup dark corn syrup
²/₃ cup light corn syrup
4 eggs, lightly beaten
³/₄ cup sugar
¹/₃ cup butter, melted
1 teaspoon vanilla
¹/₈ teaspoon salt
1 ¹/₃ cups chopped pecans
1 cup pecan halves
Pie Crust for One-Crust Pie, unbaked (see recipe on page 127)

1. Preheat oven to 325° F.

2. Mix together all of the filling ingredients, except the pecan halves, in a large bowl and stir thoroughly.

3. Arrange the pecan halves in a single layer in the bottom of the prepared pie crust and pour the filling into the crust. Bake about 1 hour, or until set. Allow to cool well before serving.

YIELD 1 PIE

Nana Jo's Chocolate Pie

In 1920, shortly after her marriage to Clarence Fitzpatrick, Jack Fitzpatrick's mother, Clara Jones, took a course at Fanny Farmer's Cooking School in Boston, where she acquired this recipe for chocolate pie. Although not currently offered at The Red Lion Inn, it nevertheless remains a family favorite.

2 cups milk
2 ounces unsweetened chocolate
1 cup sugar
$^1/_2$ cup flour
$^1/_2$ teaspoon salt
2 eggs, separated
2 teaspoons vanilla
Pie Crust for One-Crust Pie, baked (see recipe below)
lightly sweetened whipped cream

1. Heat $1^1/_2$ cups of the milk with the chocolate in the top of a double boiler over simmering water. Mix well until the chocolate is melted (it will remain suspended in tiny droplets in the milk).

2. Combine the sugar, flour, and salt in a small bowl. Add the remaining milk and stir to create a paste. Add the paste to the chocolate mixture in the pan and cook over medium heat, stirring until thick, about 10 minutes. Reduce heat to low, cover, and cook for 15 minutes, stirring occasionally.

3. Whisk the egg yolks slightly in a small bowl and mix in a spoonful or two of the chocolate mixture. When smooth, add the yolk mixture to the chocolate mixture and cook for 2 minutes, stirring constantly.

4. Beat the egg whites to form soft peaks. Carefully fold the beaten egg whites into the chocolate mixture until completely blended. Allow to cool, then add the vanilla. (The filling may be refrigerated for 24 hours at this point.)

5. Pour the filling into the prepared pie crust. Chill and serve with the whipped cream.

YIELD 1 PIE

Pie Crust for One-Crust Pie

¹/₄ cup cold butter
¹/₄ cup vegetable shortening
1 cup plus 2 tablespoons flour
¹/₂ teaspoon salt
¹/₄ cup cold milk

1. Blend the butter and shortening together with a wooden spoon in a small bowl.

2. Sift together the flour and salt in a large bowl. Cut in the butter and shortening mixture, using a pastry blender or two knives, until the mixture resembles cornmeal. Add the cold milk and blend until absorbed. (Or, if using a food processor, place the butter, shortening, flour, and salt in the bowl, fitted with a steel blade. Process until the mixture reaches the consistency of cornmeal. With the processor on, add the milk slowly through the funnel until the dough forms a ball.)

3. Roll the dough into a ball. Wrap in plastic wrap and refrigerate until chilled, about 30 minutes.

4. When ready to bake the pie crust, preheat oven to 400° F. To bake a one-crust pie crust, fit the crust into the pie plate and flute the edge. Prick the bottom and sides of the crust with a fork.

5. If the crust will be filled with a cream filling that will not be baked further, place a piece of parchment paper the size of the pie plate inside the crust, then scatter pie weights or beans on the bottom to weight it. This helps the crust to retain its shape. The crust should be baked at 400° until the fluted edge is golden brown, about 8-10 minutes. The weights and parchment should be removed after 5 minutes of baking.

6. If the crust will receive a filling that requires further baking, the crust should be prebaked for 5 minutes only, without the addition of the parchment paper and weights.

YIELD 1 CRUST

Carrot Cake

2 cups vegetable oil
2 ²/₃ cups sugar
6 eggs
1 teaspoon vanilla
2 ²/₃ cups flour
2 ¹/₂ teaspoons baking powder
4 ¹/₂ teaspoons baking soda
¹/₂ teaspoon salt
2 teaspoons ground cinnamon
2 ²/₃ cups grated carrots
¹/₂ cup canned crushed pineapple, well drained
1 ³/₄ cups chopped walnuts
Cream Cheese Frosting (see recipe below)

1. Preheat oven to 350° F. Grease and flour two 9" round cake pans.

2. Cream together the oil and sugar in a large bowl. Add the eggs, one at a time, mixing well after each addition. Add the vanilla and cream together well.

3. Sift together the flour, baking powder, baking soda, salt, and cinnamon. Add to the creamed mixture and mix with an electric mixer for about 5 minutes. Stir in the carrots, pineapple, and walnuts.

4. Pour the batter into the prepared cake pans and bake for 40-45 minutes, or until a toothpick inserted in the center comes out clean. Allow the layers to cool in the pans on a wire rack for 5 minutes, then remove the layers from the pans by inverting onto the wire rack and continue to cool.

5. Place one cake layer on a plate and spread the prepared *Cream Cheese Frosting* evenly over the top. Set the second layer on top of the first and spread the frosting on the sides of the layers and over the top.

SERVES 10-12

Cream Cheese Frosting

¹/₄ cup butter, at room temperature
¹/₄ cup cream cheese, at room temperature

1 pound confectioners' sugar, sifted
1 teaspoon vanilla
2-4 tablespoons milk

     Beat together the butter and cream cheese in a large bowl with an electric mixer. Add the sugar, vanilla, and 2 tablespoons of the milk and mix until a good spreading consistency. Add more milk if necessary.

YIELD FROSTING FOR 1 DOUBLE-LAYER CAKE

Vlad Beliavskii drew this thank-you cartoon in The Red Lion Inn's guest book when the Kiev Chamber Orchestra visited the Berkshires in 1995.

Chocolate Devil's Food Cake

3 cups cake flour, sifted
2 cups sugar
1 cup unsweetened cocoa
$^1/_2$ teaspoon salt
2 teaspoons baking soda
1 cup sour cream

1 $^1/_4$ cups vegetable oil
1 cup hot water
2 eggs
1 tablespoon vanilla
Dark Chocolate Buttercream Icing
(see recipe below)

1. Preheat oven to 350° F. Grease and flour two 10" round cake pans.

2. Sift together all of the dry ingredients. Set aside.

3. Mix together the sour cream, oil, hot water, eggs, and vanilla in a large bowl. Beat in the reserved dry ingredients and mix thoroughly.

4. Pour the batter into the prepared cake pans and bake for 30-35 minutes, or until a toothpick inserted in the center comes out clean. Allow the layers to cool in the pans on a wire rack for 5 minutes, then remove the layers from the pans by inverting onto wire racks and continue to cool.

5. Place one cake layer on a plate and spread the prepared *Dark Chocolate Buttercream Icing* evenly over the top. Set the second layer on top of the first and spread the icing on the sides of the layers and over the top.

YIELD 1 DOUBLE-LAYER CAKE

Dark Chocolate Buttercream Icing

1 $^1/_2$ cups butter, at room temperature
1 cup plus 2 tablespoons unsweetened cocoa
4 cups confectioners' sugar
$^1/_2$ cup plus 2 tablespoons milk
1 $^1/_2$ teaspoons vanilla

Cream the butter well in a large bowl. Cream in the remaining ingredients, beating well. If the icing is too thick to spread, add more milk.

YIELD ICING FOR 1 DOUBLE-LAYER CAKE

Cheesecake with New England Blueberry Sauce

Crust:
1 ¹/₂ cups graham cracker crumbs
¹/₄ cup sugar
¹/₃ cup butter, melted

Filling:
1 ¹/₂ pounds cream cheese, at room temperature (3 large packages)
1 ¹/₂ cups sugar
6 eggs, at room temperature
2 cups sour cream, at room temperature
2 tablespoons cornstarch
1 tablespoon fresh lemon juice
2 teaspoons vanilla
New England Blueberry Sauce (see recipe below)

1. Preheat oven to 350° F. Lightly grease a 10" springform pan.

2. For the crust: Combine the graham cracker crumbs and sugar in a bowl. Add the melted butter and mix until all of the crumbs are moistened.

3. Press the mixture into the prepared pan, thoroughly covering the bottom and pressing the mixture to the top of the sides. Bake for 10 minutes. Remove from oven and allow to cool for at least 10 minutes.

4. For the filling: Cream together the cream cheese and sugar in a large bowl with an electric mixer. Mix in the remaining ingredients, except the blueberry sauce, and beat at medium speed for 2-3 minutes, scraping the bowl once.

5. Pour the filling into the cooled crust and bake for 40 minutes, gently rotating the pan once during the baking. Turn off oven heat and leave the cheesecake in the oven for 30-45 minutes more until set, rotating the pan twice. Then remove the cheesecake from the oven and allow to cool thoroughly. Cover and chill overnight or for at least 3 hours.

6. Pour the prepared *New England Blueberry Sauce* on top of the cheesecake before serving, spreading to cover the center.

SERVES 10-12

CHAPTER 11

Puddings, Pastries & Desserts

There are grunts, duffs, flummeries, pandowdies, bettys, slumps, cobblers, fools, buckles, syllabubs, and tansies — all quaint, old-fashioned names that often confound us today. Were our foremothers playing word tricks, knowing future generations would never break the secret code?

Even leading food writers disagree on exact directions for making these revered desserts. A grunt, for example, according to the editors of *The American Heritage Cookbook,* is made by cooking the fruit, pouring it in a baking dish, dropping biscuit dough on top, covering it tightly, and placing it in a pan of hot water in a heated oven where it will steam for one and a half hours. Betty Crocker agrees, but James Beard says a grunt is baked, and not steamed, and the editors of Time-Life's *American Cooking: New England* insist that it's made just like a slump, in which the fruit is cooked on top of the stove, then it's topped with spoon-

fuls of biscuit dough, covered, and cooked for thirty minutes more.

There's just as much controversy over flummeries. In her *New England Cookbook,* Eleanor Early says to line a loaf pan with slices of bread and then to alternate cooked berries with buttered slices of bread, ending with a piece of bread. It's then baked in the oven. The editors of *The American Heritage Cookbook,* however, describe a concoction similar to a custard, attributing it to the Shakers, who, by the way, had many settlements near Stockbridge; this cookbook claims that the Shakers developed flummeries for the aged in their community, who had difficulty chewing. Their version is a cold, molded custard dish that incorporates berries and that is generally topped with whipped cream and additional sweetened berries.

Syllabub seems to have several interpretations as well. In some instances, it's referred to as an eggnog-type drink made with wine, and in others, it's served as a thicker custard-style pudding. For an exercise in the absolutely ridiculous, however, few recipes can top the one for syllabub that the normally very reasonable Amelia Simmons included in *American Cookery* in 1796. She makes a pudding and then recommends milking a cow directly into the dessert to make it light, airy, and frothy. This may be an idea that she adapted from Richard Brigg's *New Art of Cookery*, a 1792 book published in Philadelphia, which was a reprint of an English cookbook. It advised readers to fill a bowl with wine and place it under a cow for milking "til the Syllabub has a fine froth at the top."

Similarly, cobblers are confused with pandowdies, but the dish known as fool is universally described as fruit cooked on the stove until very tender and then pureed and cooled before it is folded into whipped cream.

The Red Lion Inn's *Blackberry Tansey* is much more sensible than syllabub. It's a scrumptious concoction that starts with berries cooked on the stove and ends as a baked dish topped with bread crumbs — and it's as pretty as it is good.

Traditionally, Americans now eat their puddings after dinner as a sweet finale, but in Merry Olde England, steamed puddings preceded the main dish — and that was the practice of early New Englanders as well. According to Hilde Gabriel Lee in *Taste of the States: A Food History of America*, the first Thanksgiving started with a baked Indian whortleberry pudding. By the mid-eighteenth century, however, the progressive Democrats, who considered themselves quite the reformers, were serving their puddings at the end of the meal, while the Federalists clung to the traditional English manner of serving them at the beginning. As with the Revolutionary War, the reformers eventually won out.

Some desserts at The Red Lion Inn follow the homey, comfortable pattern of the desserts served in the homes of early settlers. Others, however, reflect the modern twentieth-century revolution in dining that has propelled the inn into the twenty-first century.

"Aunt Mert" Plumb, co-owner with her husband Charles, and later their nephews, from 1862 to 1952, used a handwritten cookbook in The Red Lion Inn's kitchen. Her recipe for the thrifty New England favorite that she called Mother's Indian Pudding probably originated some time prior to 1879 and reads "3 cups molasses, 5 cups flour, 1 cup sour milk, 2T ginger, ²/₃ cup butter, and 2 eggs."

Indian Pudding

Indian pudding is the oldest of New England desserts, and many people think that it is the best. Early New Englanders baked it on Saturday, in the same oven as the baked beans. The pudding cooked for ten hours in the oven and was eaten for supper, dished up in a soup plate and drowned in thick, sweet cream. Here is the very old, very New England, very Red Lion Inn version, which fortunately takes only two hours to cook. Indian pudding is best if made a day before it is eaten.

6 cups milk
$^1/_2$ cup butter
$^1/_2$ cup plus 2 tablespoons cornmeal
2 eggs
2 $^2/_3$ cups molasses
3 tablespoons ground cinnamon
1 tablespoon ground ginger
1 cup peeled, cored, and thinly sliced apples
$^1/_2$ cup raisins
vanilla ice cream or whipped cream, for topping

1. Preheat oven to 300° F. Grease a $2^1/_2$-3-quart shallow baking dish.

2. Combine 5 cups of the milk with the butter in a large saucepan and bring just to a boil.

3. Mix together the remaining milk with the cornmeal in a bowl and add to the scalded milk. Cook for 20 minutes over low heat, stirring slowly so the mixture does not burn.

4. Mix together the eggs, molasses, and spices in a bowl. Add the egg mixture to the thickened cornmeal mixture, whisking thoroughly. Pour the mixture into the prepared baking dish and bake for 1 hour.

5. Stir the apples and raisins into the pudding and bake for 1 hour more, or until a toothpick inserted in the center comes out clean. Serve warm, topped with either topping.

SERVES 10-12

Red Lion Inn Bread Pudding

1 loaf white bread (1 pound), cubed (crusts removed)
4 cups milk
7 eggs
1 teaspoon vanilla
1 ¼ cups sugar
¼ cup raisins

1. Preheat oven to 300° F. Grease an 8" square baking pan.

2. Place the bread cubes in the prepared pan.

3. Mix together the milk, eggs, vanilla, and sugar and pour over the bread. Press down on the bread with a spoon until thoroughly saturated with the liquid and bake for 20 minutes.

4. Stir the pudding and sprinkle the raisins over the top. Press the pudding down to cover the raisins with liquid. Bake for 1 hour 30 minutes more, or until a knife inserted in the center (all the way to the bottom of the pan) comes out clean. Serve warm.

SERVES 8

Rice Pudding

¹/₂ cup uncooked white rice
2 ¹/₂ cups water
¹/₈ teaspoon salt
1 can sweetened condensed milk (16 ounces)
1 egg, beaten
1 teaspoon vanilla
2 tablespoons raisins
whipped cream (if served cold)
dash ground nutmeg (if served cold)

1. Combine the rice, water, and salt in the top of a double boiler and place the pan directly on the heat. Bring to a boil, cover, and simmer until the water is almost absorbed, about 35-40 minutes.

2. Add the milk and egg to the rice, stirring well. Place the pan over simmering water and cook, continuing to stir, until thickened but still creamy, about 10 minutes. Allow to cool slightly.

3. Stir the vanilla and raisins into the rice. Serve warm or serve chilled, topped with the whipped cream and nutmeg.

SERVES 8

Spiced Tapioca

1 egg, beaten
2 tablespoons quick-cooking tapioca
$1/_4$ cup sugar
$1/_8$ teaspoon salt
2 cups milk
$1/_2$ teaspoon vanilla
$1/_2$ teaspoon ground cinnamon
$1/_8$ teaspoon ground nutmeg

1. Place the beaten egg in the top of a double boiler over simmering water. Immediately add the tapioca, sugar, salt, and milk and stir well. Cook, stirring frequently, until it thickens moderately, about 12-15 minutes. Remove from heat. Stir in the vanilla, cinnamon, and nutmeg.

2. Pour the pudding into a shallow container to cool, covering the surface with plastic wrap to prevent a skin from forming. The pudding will thicken to the consistency of mayonnaise as it cools. Serve.

SERVES 4

> *"Tapioca puddings, like cornstarch puddings, were a children's dessert in New England. So when the children grew up, they wouldn't eat them any more. When girls got to college, they called tapioca 'freshman's tears' and cornstarch 'baby's flannel petticoat.'"*
>
> — *New England Cookbook*, 1954

Grape-Nut Pudding

4 cups milk
²/₃ cup Grape-Nut cereal (not flakes)
²/₃ cup sugar
dash salt
2 eggs, beaten
vanilla ice cream, whipped cream, or yogurt, for topping

1. Preheat oven to 350° F. Grease an 8" square baking pan.

2. Place the milk in a large saucepan and bring just to a boil.

3. Mix together the cereal, sugar, and salt in a bowl. Add the mixture to the scalded milk and cook over medium heat for 2-3 minutes. Remove from heat and stir one-fourth of the hot milk into the beaten eggs and mix thoroughly. Pour the eggs back into the saucepan and return the mixture to the heat, stirring constantly until thickened, about 10 minutes.

4. Pour the pudding into the prepared pan and bake for 30 minutes. Stir and serve warm with any of the toppings.

SERVES 6

Crème Caramel

³/₄ cup sugar
2 ¹/₂ tablespoons water
1 egg yolk
3 eggs
1 teaspoon vanilla
¹/₄ teaspoon ground nutmeg
3 cups milk
¹/₂ cup plus 2 tablespoons sugar
¹/₈ teaspoon salt

1. Preheat oven to 300° F.

2. Combine the ³/₄ cup sugar and the water in a heavy saucepan and cook over high heat, stirring constantly, until golden and caramelized, about 5 minutes. Pour the caramel into 6 custard cups, gently swirling to coat the bottoms. Allow the caramel to harden in the cups.

3. Whisk together the egg yolk, eggs, vanilla, and nutmeg in a bowl. Add the milk, the ¹/₂ cup plus 2 tablespoons sugar, and the salt and blend well.

4. Evenly fill the custard cups with the egg mixture. Set the custard cups in a pan filled with water that comes halfway up the sides of the cups. Place the pan in the oven and bake for 20 minutes. Revolve the pan 180 degrees and bake for 35-45 minutes more, or until a knife inserted down the side of the custard comes out clean. Serve.

SERVES 6

Blackberry Tansey

This dish is equally good with blueberries, but with blueberries, you should substitute 1 tablepoon fresh lemon juice for 1 tablespoon berry juice.

2 cups fresh blackberries
1 tablespoon water
¹/₄ teaspoon ground nutmeg
1 tablespoon cornstarch
2 eggs
¹/₂ cup sugar
2 tablespoons butter, melted
2 cups dried bread crumbs
vanilla ice cream or whipped cream, for topping

1. Preheat oven to 350° F. Grease an 8" square baking pan or a 10" pie plate.

2. Rinse the blackberries in cold water, removing any impurities. Combine the blackberries and water in a saucepan and cook gently over low heat until light purple and juicy, about 6 minutes.

3. Remove ¹/₂ cup of the berry juice and combine with the nutmeg and cornstarch in another saucepan. Cook over medium heat, stirring constantly, until thickened, about 5 minutes. Add the cooked berries and any remaining juice and stir together.

4. Beat together the eggs, sugar, and melted butter in a bowl until blended. Add the bread crumbs and toss to moisten.

5. Pour the blackberry mixture into the prepared pan. Spoon the bread crumb mixture over the top and bake until lightly browned on top, about 20-30 minutes. Serve warm with either topping.

SERVES 6

Apple Crisp

Jane Fitzpatrick contributed this cherished family recipe to the inn. If apples are not available, peaches or pears are excellent substitutes, and fresh berries, especially fresh-from-the-vine blackberries are a wonderful addition.

4 cups cored, peeled, and sliced Cortland or other tart apples (about 6-8 apples)
¹/₂ cup water
³/₄ cup flour
¹/₂ cup sugar
¹/₂ cup firmly packed light brown sugar
1 teaspoon ground cinnamon
¹/₂ teaspoon salt
¹/₂ cup butter, at room temperature
vanilla ice cream or whipped cream, for topping

1. Preheat oven to 350° F. Grease a deep baking dish.
2. Arrange the apple slices in the prepared dish and pour the water over the slices.
3. Stir together the flour, both sugars, the cinnamon, and salt in a bowl. Cut in the butter with a pastry blender or fork until the mixture resembles tiny pebbles. Spread the topping over the apples and bake until the apples are tender and the crust is brown, about 35-45 minutes. Serve warm with either topping.

SERVES 6

Louisa May Alcott, author of Little Women, loved slump so much that she named her house in Concord, Massachusetts "Apple Slump."

Apple-Cranberry Crisp

1 cup rolled oats
1 cup flour
1 cup firmly packed light brown sugar
$1/_4$ teaspoon baking soda
$1/_4$ teaspoon baking powder
$1/_4$ teaspoon salt
$1/_2$ cup butter, melted
$3 1/_2$ pounds tart apples, peeled, cored, and sliced (about 7 large apples)
$1/_2$ cup fresh cranberries
$3/_4$ cup sugar
$1 1/_2$ teaspoons ground cinnamon

1. Preheat oven to 350° F. Grease just the bottom of an 8" square baking pan.

2. Mix together the oats, flour, brown sugar, baking soda, baking powder, and salt in a large bowl. Add the melted butter and blend well, until all of the dry ingredients are moistened.

3. Combine the apple slices and cranberries in another large bowl. Add the sugar and cinnamon and toss well.

4. Place one-third of the oat mixture in the prepared pan and press the mixture down. Pour in the apple-cranberry mixture. Cover with the remaining oat mixture. Cover the pan with aluminum foil and bake until the apples are tender, about 1 hour 15 minutes, removing the foil during the last quarter hour of cooking to brown the top. Serve warm.

SERVES 8-10

The Red Lion Inn Brownies are studded with nuts

The back portion of the Main Dining Room is often used for private parties.

This decadent Chocolate Chip Pie with Hot Fudge Sauce has long been a Red Lion Inn favorite.

Indian Pudding warmed the tummies of early New Englanders just as it does guests of The Red Lion Inn today.

A variety of flags fly above the porch at The Red Lion Inn.

The front porch at harvest time.

Roast Long Island Duckling with Cranberry Glaze.

A private and seductive booth in the Widow Bingham's Tavern.

Roast Turkey Red Lion Inn with Bread Stuffing and Pan Gravy.

Crab and Cod Cakes with Rémoulade and Corn Relish offer a new-millennium take on this old classic.

This stained-glass window hangs in the Widow Bingham's Tavern.

Chicken-Mushroom Pot Pie.

Breakfast is served every morning in the Dining Room.

These Buttermilk Apple Pancakes are a tasty variation of the recipe for Buttermilk Pancakes with Blueberries, which is found in this book.

This comfortable corner in The Parlor includes a copy of Norman Rockwell's painting, Family Tree, as well as a corner cabinet filled with Colonial china.

Drinks at The Red Lion Inn: Clockwise from top: Bloody Mary, Irish Coffee, Bingham's Blush.

This quaint sign (probably from Great Britain) hangs in the Widow Bingham's Tavern.

The Red Lion Inn has a notable wine cellar, and it is the recipient of the Wine Spectator's
Award of Excellence.

A window table in the Widow Bingham's Tavern.

Porch rockers await the holiday season.

Antique furniture and more cabinets filled with china grace The Back Parlor at The Red Lion Inn.

Baked Apples Red Lion

¹/₂ cup water
3 tablespoons bourbon
¹/₂ cup raisins
¹/₂ cup golden raisins
6 tart apples, cored and peeled halfway down
3 tablespoons butter
2 tablespoons flour
¹/₂ cup firmly packed light brown sugar
¹/₂ teaspoon vanilla
vanilla ice cream or brandy-flavored whipped cream, for topping

1. Preheat oven to 425° F. Grease a baking dish with sides at least 1" high, large enough to hold 6 apples.

2. Combine the water and bourbon in a small bowl and soak all of the raisins in the liquid until plump, about 2-3 hours. Stuff the raisins into the apple cavities.

3. Melt the butter in a saucepan. Stir in the flour and cook gently for 2 minutes. Remove from heat and stir in the brown sugar and vanilla. Spread the sugar mixture over the top of the apples.

4. Place the apples in the prepared dish and bake until a crust is set on top, about 20 minutes. Lower temperature to 350° and bake until the apples are tender, about 30 minutes more. Serve warm with either topping.

SERVES 6

CHAPTER 12

Cookies & Candies

James Beard in *American Cookery* comments: "The New York Dutch were probably the first to popularize "koekjes," [which were] baked in outdoor ovens, in ovens built into the side of the fireplace, or on a griddle set over hot coals. But obviously cookies were difficult to bake until the wood-burning or coal-fired kitchen ranges were in general use. They became a standard item for lunch boxes and for snacks, and so constant was the demand that the cookie jar or tin was brought into fashion."

There are basically six types of cookies: molded or pressed, bar, refrigerator, drop, rolled, and no-bake. Cookies are fun to make, and since they take little time to bake, are a sense of instant gratification. They are the first thing that most children try their hand at and, because cookies are basically foolproof, the sense of accomplishment leads children to try ever more complicated dishes.

According to the editors of *The American Heritage Cookbook:* "New England

cooks had a penchant for giving odd names to their cookies — apparently for no other reason than the fun of saying them. Snickerdoodles come from a tradition of this sort that includes Graham Janes, Jolly Boys, Brambles, Tangle Breeches, and Kinkawoodles."

About candies, James Beard said: "Candies had very modest beginnings in this country. The sugaring-off period in New England provided one of the principal sweets, maple sugar, and sorghums and molasses were combined with various ingredients for taffies and other simple candies. There was no efficient way to gauge cooking temperatures, essential in candy making, so the techniques for preparing more elaborate candies did not become common until the 1880s when cookbooks introduced candy or 'confectionery' chapters."

Ann Fitzpatrick Brown, Jack and Jane Fitzpatrick's youngest daughter, is creative and inventive, and she loves fantasy and whimsy. In 1975, she formed her own company, which presided over the creation of whimsical fantasies made with gumdrops, Necco wafers, a white icing, and other candies. She called the company Gum Drop Square, and she sold her confections to Bloomingdale's, Neiman-Marcus, Macy's, Filene's, and others. For Bloomingdale's, she designed a four-foot Santa Claus that she constructed in their window. It attracted the attention of Imelda Marcos, who bought it for $450 and slipped it away to her suite at the Waldorf-Astoria. For Neiman-Marcus, Ann designed a 500-pound replica of Bunratty Castle.

But Ann's most stupendous creation was for Macy's in New York City. For them, she designed a candy castle made of over one-million pieces of candy and weighing over a ton. She had to ship it to New York in eight pieces.

Ann also designed a candy model of the U.S. *Eagle* as a centerpiece for a dinner commemorating the end of the "Tall Ships" transatlantic race for the U.S. Bicentennial in 1976, a model of the Boston City Hall, a replica of St. Basil's Cathedral in Moscow, and a seven-foot candy statue of George Washington that weighed 282 pounds.

The Red Lion Inn prides itself on its cookie and candy edibles. The brownies and chocolate chip cookies are legendary, as are the chocolate-covered strawberries. The truffles and bourbon balls are easy confections to make at home, and the strawberry delights are attractive garnishments for other desserts.

Note: See Chapter 13, Holiday Time at The Red Lion Inn, for the recipe *Bourbon Balls*.

Replica of Main Street, Stockbridge, in candy and gumdrops – part of The Red Lion Inn's Christmas decorations.

Red Lion Inn Chocolate Chip Cookies

Along with *Red Lion Inn Brownies* (see recipe on page 153), these chocolate chip cookies top the list of requested favorites. The recipe originated with Ruth Wakefield, who ran the Toll House Restaurant in Massachusetts. She eventually sold the right to the Toll House name to the Nestlé Company, who continue to keep the name alive.

1 cup butter, at room temperature
³/₄ cup firmly packed light brown sugar
³/₄ cup sugar
2 eggs
1 teaspoon vanilla
3 cups flour
1 teaspoon baking soda
¹/₂ teaspoon salt
1 package semisweet chocolate chips (12 ounces)

1. Preheat oven to 350° F. Line a baking sheet with lightly buttered parchment paper.

2. Cream the butter in a mixing bowl. Add both sugars and blend together well. Add the eggs and vanilla, then cream thoroughly.

3. Sift together the flour, baking soda, and salt in another bowl. Stir the flour mixture into the creamed mixture. Gently stir in chocolate chips.

4. Drop the dough in 1¹/₂" balls onto the prepared baking sheet and bake until golden, about 8-12 minutes. Allow to cool slightly, about 3 minutes, on the baking sheet, then transfer to a wire rack to cool completely.

YIELD 3¹/₂ DOZEN COOKIES

Decorated Sugar Cookies

These frosted, cutout sugar cookies are ideal for a child's first attempts at baking. Christmas trees painted with bright green frosting, red hearts for Valentine's Day, and orange pumpkins for Halloween are fun to make and delight both youngsters and adults.

$^1/_2$ cup butter, at room temperature
$^3/_4$ cup sugar
2 egg yolks
$^3/_4$ teaspoon vanilla
1 tablespoon milk

1 $^1/_2$ cups flour
$^1/_4$ teaspoon salt
$^1/_4$ teaspoon baking powder
Sugar Cookie Frosting (see recipe below)

1. Cream the butter in a mixing bowl until very fluffy. Add the sugar, then cream together well. Beat in the egg yolks, vanilla, and milk.

2. Sift together the flour, salt, and baking powder in another bowl. Add the flour mixture to the creamed mixture and mix together well. Form the dough into a ball, wrap in plastic wrap, and refrigerate for at least 1 hour, or until firm.

3. Preheat oven to 350° F. Line a large baking sheet with lightly buttered parchment paper.

4. Roll out the dough to $^1/_4$" thickness on a floured surface. Flour the cookie cutters and cut out the cookies. Place the cookies on the prepared baking sheet and bake until golden, about 8-10 minutes. Remove the cookies from the sheet and place on a rack to cool. Frost the cooled cookies with the prepared *Sugar Cookie Frosting.*

YIELD 4-5 DOZEN COOKIES

Sugar Cookie Frosting

4 $^1/_2$ cups sifted confectioners' sugar
$^1/_4$ cup milk
$^1/_2$ teaspoon vanilla
food coloring (optional)

Mix together the confectioners' sugar, milk, and vanilla in a bowl. If the frosting is too thick to spread, add more milk. Add various colors of food coloring to small amounts of the frosting for decorating as desired.

YIELD 2$^1/_4$ CUPS

Oatmeal-Butterscotch Cookies

This recipe is sometimes varied at The Red Lion Inn by using currants in place of the butterscotch bits.

1 cup butter, at room temperature
1 ¹/₂ cups firmly packed light brown sugar
2 eggs
4 teaspoons water
2 ¹/₂ cups flour
2 teaspoons baking powder
1 teaspoon baking soda
1 teaspoon salt
2 cups rolled oats
2 cups butterscotch bits

1. Preheat oven to 350° F. Line a baking sheet with lightly buttered parchment paper.

2. Cream together the butter and brown sugar in a mixing bowl until fluffy. Add the eggs and water and blend together well.

3. Sift together the flour, baking powder, baking soda, and salt in another bowl. Add the flour mixture to the creamed mixture and mix together well. Stir in the oats and butterscotch bits.

4. Drop 1¹/₂" balls of the dough onto the prepared baking sheet and bake until golden, about 8-12 minutes. Allow to cool slightly on the baking sheet, about 3 minutes, then transfer to a wire rack to cool completely.

YIELD 3-4 DOZEN COOKIES

Red Lion Inn Brownies

These fudgy brownies, with a milk chocolate flavor, are among the most popular requests at The Red Lion Inn. They're often served on large silver trays as dessert for business luncheons or beside the coffee table at evening cocktail parties. They are regularly offered on the menu, topped with vanilla ice cream and *Hot Fudge Sauce,* for a chocolate lover's dream come true.

4 ounces unsweetened chocolate
$^1/_2$ cup butter
4 eggs
2 cups sugar
$^1/_4$ teaspoon salt
1 tablespoon vanilla
1 cup flour
$^3/_4$ cup chopped walnuts
vanilla ice cream (optional)
Hot Fudge Sauce (see recipe on pages 128-129)

1. Preheat oven to 350° F. Line a 9" x 12" baking pan with lightly buttered parchment paper.

2. Melt the chocolate and butter in the top of a double boiler over simmering water, stirring frequently. Remove from heat and allow to cool.

3. Beat the eggs in a mixing bowl until frothy. Add the sugar and blend together well. Gently stir in the melted chocolate mixture, the salt, and vanilla. Add the flour and walnuts and stir by hand just until blended.

4. Spread the batter in the prepared pan and bake until crusty on top and almost firm to the touch, about 30-35 minutes. Allow to cool completely in the pan. Cut into squares and serve, if desired, with a scoop of ice cream on top, covered by the prepared *Hot Fudge Sauce.*

YIELD 24 BROWNIES

Nana Pratt's Brown Sugar Squares

Nana Pratt was the mother of Jane Fitzpatrick, owner of The Red Lion Inn. Although these are not regularly served at the inn, you may find them served for special occasions.

$1/4$ cup butter, at room temperature
1 cup firmly packed light brown sugar
1 egg
$1/2$ cup chopped walnuts
1 teaspoon vanilla
$2/3$ cup flour
1 teaspoon baking powder
$1/8$ teaspoon salt

1. Preheat oven to 350° F. Grease an 8" square baking pan.
2. Cream the butter in a mixing bowl. Add the brown sugar, egg, walnuts, and vanilla and beat well.
3. Sift together the flour, baking powder, and salt in another bowl. Add the flour mixture to the creamed mixture and beat thoroughly.
4. Spread the dough in the prepared pan and bake for 30 minutes or until a toothpick inserted in the center comes out clean. Do not overbake. Allow to cool completely in the pan. Cut into squares and serve.

YIELD 9-12 SQUARES

Hermits

3 cups flour
1 1/4 cups sugar
1/2 teaspoon salt
1 1/2 teaspoons baking soda
1 teaspoon ground cloves
1 teaspoon ground ginger
1 teaspoon ground cinnamon
1/2 cup vegetable oil
1 egg
1/4 cup molasses
5 tablespoons water
1/2 cup raisins

1. Preheat oven to 350° F. Grease a 9" x 13" baking pan.

2. Sift together the flour, sugar, salt, baking soda, cloves, ginger, and cinnamon in a mixing bowl.

3. Mix together the oil, egg, molasses, and water in another bowl. Add the oil mixture to the flour mixture and mix together well. Stir in the raisins. The dough will be thick, so could mix with hands.

4. Spread the dough in the prepared pan and bake for 20 minutes. Allow to cool completely in the pan. Cut into squares and serve.

YIELD 12 SQUARES

Jacks Oatmeal Cookie Sandwich

These cookies are one of the popular dessert offerings at Jacks Grill in Housatonic, a village about 5 miles south of Stockbridge. Housatonic is where the Fitzpatrick's Housatonic Curtain Company is located — the place where many of the curtains for Country Curtains are made. The charming restaurant, named for Jack Fitzpatrick and featuring his favorite truck as a logo, is casual and fun.

1 cup butter
1 ¹/₂ cups firmly packed brown sugar
³/₄ cup sugar
2 eggs
¹/₄ cup water
2 ¹/₂ cups flour
³/₄ teaspoon baking powder
³/₄ teaspoon baking soda
³/₄ teaspoon salt
1 ¹/₂ teaspoons vanilla
4 ¹/₂ cups rolled oats
Ben & Jerry's Chunky Monkey Ice Cream
Chocolate Sauce (see recipe below)

1. Preheat oven to 375° F. Line a baking sheet with parchment paper.

2. Cream the butter in a mixing bowl with an electric mixer. Add both sugars, the eggs, and water, then cream together until well blended.

3. Sift together the flour, baking powder, baking soda, and salt in a bowl. Add the flour mixture to the creamed mixture and blend together well. Add the vanilla and oats and mix together (may have to blend with hands if dough becomes too stiff for electric mixer).

4. Drop the batter by tablespoonfuls onto the prepared baking sheet and bake until golden brown, about 8-10 minutes. Allow to cool on the baking sheet, about 3 minutes, then transfer to a wire rack to cool completely.

5. Allow the ice cream to soften slightly. Place a cookie on a plate. Spread the ice cream on the cookie, then top with another cookie.

6. Pour 2 tablespoons of the prepared *Chocolate Sauce* on a dessert plate and top with an ice-cream sandwich. Serve immediately.

YIELD ABOUT 20 SANDWICHES

Chocolate Sauce

1 1/2 cups heavy cream
15 ounces semisweet chocolate chips

Heat the cream in a saucepan to a slow simmer. Remove from heat and whisk in the chocolate chips until smooth. This sauce may be prepared up to 1 week in advance and stored in the refrigerator.

YIELD 2 1/2 CUPS

Main Street, Housatonic, Mass. 01236

Whoopie Pies

6 tablespoons vegetable shortening
1 cup sugar
1 egg
1 cup milk
1 teaspoon vanilla
2 cups flour

1 $^{1}/_{2}$ teaspoons baking soda
$^{1}/_{2}$ teaspoon salt
$^{1}/_{2}$ cup unsweetened cocoa
1 tablespoon vegetable oil
Fluffy Vanilla Filling (see recipe below)

1. Preheat oven to 350° F. Line a baking sheet with parchment paper.

2. Cream together the shortening, sugar, egg, milk, and vanilla in a mixing bowl.

3. Mix together the flour, baking soda, salt, cocoa, and oil in another bowl. Add the flour mixture to the creamed mixture and blend together well.

4. Drop the batter by spoonfuls onto the prepared baking sheet, spacing 2" apart, and bake until done, about 8-10 minutes. Allow to cool slightly on the baking sheet, about 3 minutes, then transfer to a wire rack to cool completely.

5. To assemble a "pie," spread some of the prepared *Fluffy Vanilla Frosting* on one chocolate cookie and top with a second cookie. Repeat, using all of the cookies and filling.

YIELD 18 PIES

Fluffy Vanilla Filling

5 tablespoons flour
1 cup milk
$^{1}/_{2}$ cup butter, at room temperature
$^{1}/_{2}$ cup vegetable shortening
1 cup sugar
1 teaspoon salt
1 teaspoon vanilla

1. Blend together the flour and milk in a saucepan and cook over medium heat until thick, about 2-3 minutes. Allow to cool.

2. Cream together the butter and shortening in a mixing bowl with an electric mixer. Add the sugar, salt, and the cooled milk mixture and beat on high speed until fluffy, about 8 minutes. Blend in the vanilla.

YIELD 3 CUPS

Chocolate Truffles

2 cups semisweet chocolate chips
³/₄ cup sweetened condensed milk
1 ¹/₂ teaspoons vanilla
pinch salt
1 cup chopped packaged flaked coconut

1. Melt the chocolate in the top of a double boiler over simmering water. Remove from heat and add the milk, vanilla, and salt, stirring until well blended. Chill until firm enough to handle, about 1 hour.

2. Grease hands with butter. Shape the dough into 1" balls and roll in the coconut. Chill for 1 hour before serving.

YIELD 36 TRUFFLES

Chocolate-Covered Strawberries

1 quart fresh strawberries, stems and leaves removed
1 cup semisweet chocolate chips (6 ounces)
1 1/2 teaspoons butter
2 tablespoons milk or light cream

1. Rinse the strawberries in cold water and pat dry with paper towels.

2. Melt the chocolate chips and butter in the top of a double boiler over low heat.

3. While the chocolate is melting, heat the milk in a saucepan over low heat, until warm. When the chocolate is melted, gently stir in the warm milk. Thin with more milk if the chocolate remains too thick for dipping.

4. Holding the strawberries at the top, dip in the chocolate, covering about three-fourths of the strawberry. Immediately place the strawberries on a chilled plate that has been lightly oiled with vegetable oil. Chill in the refrigerator until the chocolate has hardened. The strawberries should be served on the day that they are made.

SERVES 12-15

Strawberry Delights

These confections might be used as decorative garnishments to accompany stemmed glasses of sherbets, ices, and ice cream, or as a pretty accompaniment to numerous other dishes.

1 can sweetened condensed milk (14 ounces)
5 ¹/₄ cups packaged flaked coconut
²/₃ cup strawberry gelatin powder (two 3-ounce packages)
1 cup ground blanched almonds (see page 26)
1 teaspoon almond extract
red food coloring
2 ¹/₂ cups confectioners' sugar
3 tablespoons cream
green food coloring

1. Line a baking sheet with parchment paper.

2. Combine the milk, coconut, ¹/₃ cup of the gelatin powder, the almonds, almond extract, and red food coloring in a mixing bowl and stir together well. Cover and chill in the refrigerator until stiff enough to shape, about 1 hour.

3. Divide the dough into ¹/₂ tablespoon balls and roll into strawberry shapes. Roll the dough "strawberries" in the remaining gelatin powder and place on the prepared baking sheet.

4. Cream together the confectioners' sugar, cream, and green food coloring in a bowl. Place the mixture in a pastry bag, fitted with a leaf tip, and pipe leaves onto the "strawberries." Chill for 1 hour before serving.

YIELD 5 DOZEN

CHAPTER 13

Holiday Time at The Red Lion Inn

Turkeys are always associated with Thanksgiving — from that first Pilgrim celebration to today. Edward Winslow described the first Thanksgiving in 1621 thusly: "Our harvest being gotten in, our governor sent four men on fowling, that so we might, after a special manner, rejoice together after we had gathered the fruit of our labors. They four in one day killed as much fowl as, with a little help beside, served the company almost a week. At which time, among other recreations, we exercised our arms, many of the Indians coming among us, and amongst the rest their greatest king, Massasoit, with some ninety men, whom for three days we. . . feasted. And they went out and killed five deer, which they brought to the plantation and bestowed on our Governor and upon the Captain and others."

This description may sound like a magnificent feast, but according to *American Cooking: New England*: "The first Thanks-

giving is often depicted as a lavish feast, with outdoor tables laden with all sorts of delicacies, but it could not have been anything of the sort. Plymouth at that time was a tiny cluster of huts, built mostly of sod and thatch. The colonists had few possessions beyond the simplest tools and household equipment, and the stores they had brought from England were practically exhausted. Most likely they entertained their Indian friends with fish and game, including the deer that the guests contributed, and corn and beans cooked in the Indian manner."

But as ingredients multiplied and the tools needed for cooking and baking improved, the variety of Thanksgiving dishes increased. Pies became extraordinarily popular, and they were made in enormous quantities. Harriet Beecher Stowe wrote in her book *Oldtown Folks, A Story of New England* that Thanksgiving pies were made in "forties, fifties, and hundred" and made of "everything in the earth and under the earth . . . pumpkins, cranberries, huckle-berries, cherries, green currants, peaches, pears, plums, custards, apples . . . pies with top crusts and pies without, pies adorned with all sorts of fanciful fluting and architectural strips. . . ."

Holiday time at The Red Lion Inn is eagerly anticipated. The tree stands in the center of the lobby heavily laden with precious ornaments that the Fitzpatricks have collected over the years — many given to them by guests — and the china cabinets are filled with Mrs. Fitzpatrick's collection of nativity scenes. Inside and out, it's a lavish holiday display that frequently includes musical performances.

In addition, Ann Fitzpatrick Brown, Jack and Jane Fitzpatrick's daughter, once owned a company called Gum Drop Square (see Chapter 12, Cookies & Candies), and the inn is fortunate to have several of Ann's candy sculptures. Notable among them is a candy replica of Main Street in Stockbridge, a candy castle, a three and a half-foot gum-drop Santa Clause, and a twelve-foot candy train. These are refreshed every year and come out for display at Christmas, where they continue to delight young and old alike. The staff of the inn wisely accompanies the sculptures with glass bowls of gumdrops to divert curious fingers that might otherwise pluck one from Santa's big tummy.

Of considerable pride also is the fact that in 1998 noted children's book author and illustrator Jan Brett updated Clement Moore's classic poem *The Night Before Christmas* with her charming illustrations that feature Stockbridge and The Red Lion Inn in the background. When she autographed copies at The Red Lion Inn in December 1998, the lines stretched from the Side Parlor, into the Dining Room, across the Lobby, and outside onto the porch. In 1999, she wrote and illustrated an original children's book titled *Gingerbread Baby*, and she used Alexander Brown, Ann Fitzpatrick Brown's son, as the model.

"Bless, O Lord, the food we eat
And the cooks who give it taste
And all the bar-b-quers here
Hungry for the baste.

Bless, O Lord, your servants
Whose names are Jane and Jack
Before they're glazed with spice and sauce
Upon the roasting rack.

Give, O Lord, their Minister
Two sermons to which they'll cleave.
For all they need is two a year:
On Easter and Christmas Eve.

So, Lord, make us merry
And smell the delicious laughter.
And bless us every one tonight
And forever after.

— penned by Elizabeth Wheeler for a Fitzpatrick Roast on May 21, 1994

Roast Christmas Goose with Orange Gravy

A fat goose was the traditional English Michaelmas fare from the time of Elizabeth I and later became a Christmas tradition as well. The Red Lion Inn's Christmas goose recreates that beloved early tradition.

1 goose (12-14 pounds)
2 large onions, coarsely chopped
2 oranges, peeled and sectioned
2 lemons, peeled and sectioned
2 McIntosh apples, unpeeled, cored, and quartered
3 bay leaves
salt and black pepper
boiling water
$1/_2$ cup white wine
Goose Demi-Glace (see recipe below)
Orange Gravy (see recipe below)
Apple-Apricot Chestnut Dressing (see recipe below)

1. Preheat oven to 350° F.

2. Remove the neck, liver, giblets, heart, and all fat from the goose cavity. Thoroughly rinse out the cavity and pat dry. Singe off any feathers.

3. Combine the onions, oranges, lemons, apples, and bay leaves in a bowl, then place the mixture in the goose cavity. Season with salt and black pepper. (This dressing is for seasoning only. It will not be served.)

4. Truss the bird to hold the legs together. Prick the skin well around the legs and back (this will allow the fat to drain during cooking). Rub the skin well with the salt and black pepper. Place the goose on a rack in a roasting pan.

5. Roast the goose for approximately 12 minutes per pound, about 2 hours 30-45 minutes. Baste with the boiling water twice during the first hour to help render the fat. Drain the fat as it accumulates in the pan and reserve for the *Goose Demi-Glace.*

6. When a meat thermometer registers 180°, remove the pan from the oven and transfer the goose to a heated platter. Cover the goose with aluminum foil and let stand while preparing the *Goose Demi-Glace* and *Orange Gravy.*

7. Drain the fat from the roasting pan and reserve. Add the wine to the pan, scraping the brown bits on the bottom. Add this liquid to the demi-glace for the *Orange Gravy.*

8. To serve, carve the goose into slices and serve the gravy and the prepared *Apple-Apricot Chestnut Dressing* on the side.

SERVES 8-10

Goose Demi-Glace

1 cup goose fat (reserved drippings)
1 cup chopped onions
¹/₂ cup chopped celery
¹/₂ cup chopped carrots
1 cup flour
8 cups goose stock
5-10 sprigs fresh parsley
3 bay leaves
2 teaspoons tomato paste
¹/₂ cup white wine
salt and black pepper to taste

1. Heat the fat in a large pot. Add the vegetables and sauté over medium heat until lightly browned and syrupy, about 15 minutes. Add the flour and cook, stirring constantly, until the flour turns a nutty color, about 10 minutes.

2. Add the stock, parsley sprigs, bay leaves, tomato paste, wine, salt and black pepper and bring to a boil. Reduce heat and simmer for 1 hour 30 minutes, skimming the fat from the top, until reduced to 5 cups.

YIELD 5 CUPS

Orange Gravy

¹/₄ cup sugar
¹/₄ cup red wine vinegar
¹/₂ cup plus 3 tablespoons fresh orange juice
2 medium oranges
5 cups Goose Demi-Glace (see recipe above)
1 lemon
2 tablespoons red currant jelly
¹/₄ cup Cointreau liqueur
salt and black pepper to taste

1. Cook the sugar in a saucepan over medium heat, stirring constantly, until it melts and turns a light brown color, about 5-6 minutes. Do not burn. Remove the saucepan from the heat. Slowly add the vinegar and orange juice. The sugar will harden, but stir the mixture together thoroughly and return to the heat. As the ingredients warm, the caramel mixture will soften. Simmer until it is reduced by half, about 15 minutes.

2. Peel the oranges, removing only the zest (no white pith) and cut the peel into thin strips. Place the strips in a saucepan, cover with water, and simmer for 2 minutes. Drain and add only the peel to the sauce.

3. Add the prepared *Goose Demi-Glace* to the sauce and simmer for 10 minutes. Squeeze the juice from the oranges and lemon and add to the sauce. Stir in the jelly and liqueur and simmer for 5 minutes more. Season with the salt and black pepper.

YIELD 5-5 $\frac{1}{2}$ CUPS

Apple-Apricot Chestnut Dressing

1 cup butter or goose fat
1 cup diced onions
$\frac{1}{2}$ cup diced celery
2 cups peeled, cored, and diced McIntosh apples
6 cups cubed bread (crusts removed)
1 $\frac{1}{2}$ cups diced apricots
1 cup peeled, boiled, and chopped chestnuts
$\frac{1}{4}$ cup chopped fresh parsley
2 teaspoons salt
1 teaspoon ground paprika
$\frac{1}{4}$ cup goose stock

1. Preheat oven to 350° F. Grease a 3-quart baking dish.

2. Melt the butter in a large saucepan. Add the onions and celery and sauté over medium heat until tender, about 5 minutes. Add the apples and sauté for 2 minutes more. Remove from heat.

3. Add the bread cubes, apricots, chestnuts, parsley, salt, and paprika. Toss until the mixture is moist but not wet.

4. Place the dressing in the prepared dish and bake for 1 hour. If too dry, moisten with a little of the stock, while baking.

YIELD 8 CUPS

Roast Turkey Red Lion Inn

1 medium turkey (about 14-16 pounds)
Bread Stuffing (see recipe below)
¹/₄ cup butter or margarine
1 teaspoon salt

¹/₄ teaspoon black pepper
1 teaspoon poultry seasoning
1 teaspoon ground sage
Pan Gravy (see recipe below)

1. Preheat oven to 450° F.

2. Remove the neck, liver, giblets, etc. from the turkey. Use the liver in the stuffing and the giblets in the gravy and set aside the remaining parts. Rinse the cavity well and pat dry.

3. Stuff the turkey with the prepared *Bread Stuffing* and truss the opening.

4. Place the turkey on a rack in a roasting pan. Rub the butter over the skin. Mix together the salt, black pepper, poultry seasoning, and sage and sprinkle over the bird. Roast the turkey for 10 minutes. Reduce temperature to 350° and roast for 20-25 minutes per pound, or until a meat thermometer registers 185°, about 3 hours 15 minutes - 4 hours 15 minutes. Baste often with the pan juices.

5. If desired, cook all of the turkey parts, except the liver. Reserve the liver for the *Bread Stuffing*. Cook the parts in water to cover over low heat until tender, about 2 hours. Drain, remove the meat from the neck and finely chop all of the meat. Set aside to use in the gravy.

6. Remove the turkey from the oven and transfer to a heated platter, reserving the pan juices. Let stand, covered with aluminum foil, for 30 minutes.

7. Prepare the *Pan Gravy*. Remove the stuffing from the turkey and place in a serving dish and keep warm. Carve the turkey and serve with the stuffing and gravy.

SERVES 10

Bread Stuffing

³/₄ cup butter
1 medium onion, chopped
¹/₂ bunch celery, chopped
1 tablespoon poultry seasoning
1 ¹/₂ teaspoons dried sage
4 bay leaves
1 tablespoon garlic powder

1 tablespoon dried rosemary
dash salt and black pepper
2 teaspoons dried thyme
3-4 cups turkey stock
turkey liver (from the recipe Roast
*   Turkey Red Lion Inn)*
20 slices day-old bread, cubed

1. Preheat oven to 350° F. Grease a 2-quart baking dish.

2. Melt $^1/_2$ cup of the butter in a large saucepan. Add all of the vegetables and seasonings and cook over medium heat until tender, about 5 minutes.

3. Add the stock and bring to a boil. Gently boil for 30 minutes. Adjust the seasonings and remove the bay leaves.

4. Melt the remaining butter in a sauté pan. Add the livers and sauté over medium heat until cooked through, about 5 minutes. Drain off fat and finely chop the livers.

5. Place the bread cubes and cooked livers in a large bowl. Add 2 cups of the hot stock with vegetables and mix together well. Add the remaining hot stock with vegetables, $^1/_2$ cup at a time, just until the bread cubes are thoroughly moistened (the amount of stock used depends on how dry the bread is).

6. Stuff the body and neck cavity of the turkey. Place the remaining stuffing in the prepared dish and bake until golden brown on top, about 45 minutes.

YIELD 8-10 CUPS

Pan Gravy

$^1/_4$ *cup flour*
2 cups turkey stock
1 teaspoon dried savory
1 teaspoon ground sage
salt and black pepper to taste
turkey giblets, cooked and chopped (from the
  recipe Roast Turkey Red Lion Inn)

1. Skim the fat from the turkey pan juices. Strain, separately reserving the juices and fat (should have $^1/_4$ cup fat).

2. Heat the reserved fat in a large saucepan. Stir in the flour and blend thoroughly to make a roux. Cook over low heat, stirring constantly, until light golden brown, about 5-8 minutes. Add the reserved turkey juices and the stock to the roux. Using a wire whisk, whip until smooth. Add the herbs and simmer for 30 minutes. Strain and season with the salt and black pepper. Stir in the giblets and heat through.

YIELD 2 CUPS

Mrs. Stephen Johnson Field, whose husband was from Stockbridge and was appointed a Supreme Court Justice by President Lincoln, wrote a book in 1890 entitled Statesmen's Dishes and How to Cook Them. *Her secret ingredients for a Christmas turkey:* "The turkey should be cooped up and fed some time before Christmas. Three days before it is slaughtered, it should have an English walnut forced down its throat three times a day, and a glass of sherry once a day. The meat will be deliciously tender, and have a fine nutty flavor."

Candied Yams with Bourbon

6-8 large yams or sweet potatoes
$1/_4$ cup dark corn syrup
$1/_4$ cup light corn syrup
$1/_4$ cup firmly packed light brown sugar
2 tablespoons pure maple syrup
$1/_4$ cup Kentucky bourbon
chopped fresh parsley, for garnish

1. Preheat oven to 350° F. Grease an 8" square baking dish.

2. Place the yams in a large pot with water to cover and boil just until tender, about 45 minutes. Peel the yams while still hot. Slice lengthwise, then crosswise, and allow to cool. Arrange the slices in the prepared dish.

3. Combine the remaining ingredients, except the parsley, in a bowl and mix together well. Pour the mixture over the sliced yams and bake until bubbling hot, about 30 minutes. Garnish with the parsley and serve.

SERVES 10-12

DATE	NAME		ADDRESS
December 1998	Jan Brett and Joe Hearne		The expressions on the faces of the children as they walked in the door of the Red Lion, all bedecked for Christmas is all the Christmas present we need! a treasure!
		Thank you!	

A Christmas thank-you by Jan Brett graces the Red Lion's guest ledger.

Pumpkin Pie

9 eggs
6 cups fresh pumpkin, cured or cooked (or you may substitute canned pumpkin)
3 cups evaporated milk
3 cups milk
3 cups firmly packed light brown sugar
1 tablespoon ground cinnamon
1 ¹/₂ teaspoons ground ginger
³/₄ teaspoon ground cloves
³/₄ teaspoon ground nutmeg
³/₄ teaspoon salt
2 prepared pie crusts, unbaked

1. Preheat oven to 325° F.
2. Stir together all of the filling ingredients in a large bowl.
3. Pour into the prepared pie crusts and bake for 45-60 minutes or until a thin knife inserted in the center comes out clean.

YIELD 2 PIES

"Pumpkin pie," according to The House Mother, *"if rightly made, is a thing of beauty and a joy — while it lasts. . . . Pies that cut a little less firm than a pine board, and those that run round your plate are alike to be avoided. Two inches deep is better than the thin plates one sometimes sees, that look for all the world like pumpkin flap-jacks. . . . With the pastry light, tender, and not too rich, and a generous filling of smooth spiced sweetness — a little 'trembly' as to consistency, and delicately brown on top — a perfect pumpkin pie, eaten before the life has gone out of it, is one of the real additions made by American cookery to the good things of the world."*

— *The American Heritage Cookbook,* 1964

Mincemeat Pie

Mincemeat pie is often a holiday treat at The Red Lion Inn, where its roots run deep in New England. According to Hilda Gabriel Lee in *Taste of the States: A Food History of America:* "Many New Englanders considered mincemeat pie, whose origin goes back to Europe, to be the king of dessert pies. Pioneer women made mincemeat with tiny pieces of beef and suet to which raisins, chopped apples, candied fruit, and spices were added. They moistened the mincemeat with brandy or hard cider, which acted as a preservative. The mincemeat was then stored in a stone crock until it was aged and ready for use."

¹/₂ cup boiled, then diced beef tenderloin
³/₄ cup diced suet
1 apple, peeled, cored, and finely diced
³/₄ cup firmly packed brown sugar
³/₄ teaspoon ground mace
³/₄ teaspoon ground nutmeg
³/₄ teaspoon ground cinnamon
³/₄ teaspoon ground cloves
¹/₂ teaspoon fresh lemon juice
1 teaspoon fresh orange juice

¹/₂ cup brandy
¹/₂ cup Madeira wine
salt to taste
³/₄ cup raisins
³/₄ cup currants
¹/₂ cup finely diced dried citron
peel of ¹/₂ lemon, finely grated
peel of ¹/₂ orange, finely grated
Pie Crust for Two-Crust Pie, unbaked
  (see recipe on pages 122-123)

1. Combine the beef, suet, and apple in a large mixing bowl. Mix together the brown sugar, all spices, both juices, brandy, wine, and salt in another bowl, then add to the beef mixture, stirring together well.

2. Mix together the raisins, currants, citron, and both zests in a bowl and add to the beef/spice mixture, again stirring together well.

3. Cover the bowl and refrigerate the mincemeat for at least 24 hours, or until all of the flavors have melded.

4. When ready to bake the pie, preheat oven to 350° F. Spoon the mincemeat in the prepared pie crust and fit the top crust over the filling. Crimp the top and bottom edges together and bake for 30 minutes, or until the pie is evenly golden brown on top.

YIELD 1 PIE.

Bourbon Balls

1 cup crushed vanilla wafers
1 cup confectioners' sugar, sifted
1 ¹/₂ cups finely chopped pecans
2 tablespoons unsweetened cocoa
2 tablespoons light corn syrup
¹/₄ cup bourbon
superfine sugar

1. Mix together all of the ingredients, except the superfine sugar, in a bowl.

2. With hands, shape the dough into 1" balls and roll in the superfine sugar. Arrange the balls in a single layer in a plastic dish with a lid. Cover tightly and set aside for at least 4 hours (preferably overnight) before serving.

YIELD 36 BALLS

Holiday Eggnog

The editors of *The American Heritage Cookbook* have these comments to make about eggnog: "Eggnog is descended from the English sack posset, a hot drink made with ale or with dry Spanish wine called sack. Like posset, eggnog was originally made with ale ("nog" is an English word for a strong ale), but — as it was adapted by Americans — it came to be made with more typical American liquors, like rum, bourbon, and even cider. The earliest American cookbooks relegated Eggnogs to a section of recipes for the sick and the weak." Today, the drink has become a favorite holiday treat, both for at home parties and at The Red Lion Inn.

1 ¹/₄ ounces dark rum
1 egg, beaten
1 teaspoon sugar
¹/₂ cup chilled milk
ground nutmeg

Shake the first four ingredients in a covered container with some shaved ice. Strain into a large, chilled wineglass and sprinkle with the nutmeg. Serve.

SERVES 1

The tree in the Front Parlor is part of every Red Lion Christmas.

JANNY KOWYNIA, COURTESY THE RED LION INN

Red Lion Inn Christmas Drink Glöog

The holiday season is always festive and colorful at The Red Lion Inn, where corporations and individuals host private parties. This holiday drink was created just for this special season.

2 quarts red wine
1 pint sweet vermouth
15 whole cloves
2 cinnamon sticks, 3" long
$^1/_4$ cup dried orange peel
20 cardamom seeds, crushed
1 $^1/_2$ cups slivered blanched almonds (see page 26)
1 $^1/_2$ cups raisins
$^1/_2$ pound lump sugar
1 cup vodka

1. Place all of the ingredients, except the sugar and vodka, in a saucepan and boil slowly, stirring occasionally, for 20 minutes. Place a rack over the saucepan and spread the sugar lumps out on the rack.

2. Warm the vodka in a small saucepan and pour over the sugar lumps until saturated. Carefully ignite the sugar and let melt into the glöog mixture. Stir.

3. Strain the liquid into heated mugs or punch cups and add a few of the blanched almonds and raisins to each cup. Serve. Leftover glöog can be bottled and reheated.

SERVES 10

CHAPTER 14

Let's Have Lunch
at The Red Lion Inn

Just as in Europe, dinner in early New England was eaten midday, with a much lighter meal served in the evening. The practice is still the tradition in much of Europe. Why did we vary the custom?

As farming gave way to industry, as Americans moved to ever-more-distant suburbs, as more housewives took jobs outside the home, as children's schools were located further from home, a large family midday meal became less practical — even less possible. Therefore, when the family finally congregated back at the homestead at the end of the day and Mom had time to prepare the evening meal after returning from work herself, that became the time when everyone sat at the table together and shared the day's events.

So we developed a fast-food midday ritual of sandwiches, hamburgers, hot dogs, or items on the school lunch menu, in place of the hearty farm meals of our ancestors. Nevertheless, the leisurely pace of lunch at The Red Lion Inn offers a variety of alternatives, some as hearty as in former days.

New England baked beans, for example, are standard luncheon fare. According to the editors of *The American Heritage Cookbook:* "It is for baked beans that Boston is known as Bean Town. The bean pot could be kept in the slow heat of a fireplace to serve at Saturday supper and Sunday breakfast. Housewives too busy with other chores were able to turn the baking of the beans over to a local baker. The baker called each Saturday morning to pick up the family's bean pot and take it to a community oven, usually in the cellar of a nearby tavern. The freelance baker then returned the baked beans, with a bit of brown bread, on Saturday evening."

Welsh rarebit, a traditional Red Lion favorite, was reputedly improvised when a

Welsh gentleman ran out of game for his banquet table and asked his cook to create something new. The cook produced this cheese dish, which he named — presumably to avoid calling the guests' attention to the fact that the meat supply had vanished — "rabbit." It persisted as Welsh rabbit in early American kitchens, although generally the name has now been changed to "rarebit."

The Red Lion Inn also offers such comforting lunchtime favorites as chicken pot pie (although it's now served with puff pastry instead of buttermilk biscuits), roast beef hash, creamed chicken in pastry shells, salmon cakes, and good old-fashioned New England corn fritters with fresh-from-the-vat maple syrup.

Joan Baez drew this sketch in The Red Lion Inn guest book during one of her visits.

Boston Baked Beans with Black Forest Ham & Red Lion Inn Applesauce

1 pound dried yellow eye or navy beans
¹/₂ cup diced yellow onions
1 pound salt pork
1 pound Black Forest ham, cooked and diced
¹/₂ cup molasses
¹/₃ cup ketchup
1 teaspoon salt
¹/₂ teaspoon ground mustard
2 tablespoons dark brown sugar
Red Lion Inn Applesauce (see recipe below)

1. Rinse the beans in a strainer and remove any impurities. Place the beans in an earthenware bean pot, cover with cold water, and soak for 4-6 hours, or overnight.

2. Preheat oven to 325° F. Without draining, place the beans over medium heat and bring to a boil. Reduce heat, cover, and simmer for 30 minutes.

3. Add the onions to the beans. Score the salt pork into wedges, cutting through the lean meat but not the rind. Add the salt pork and ham to the beans. Mix together the molasses, ketchup, salt, mustard, and brown sugar in a small bowl, then add the mixture to the beans. Bring to a boil.

4. Cover the pot and bake until done, about 6-8 hours, watching that the beans don't get too dry. If necessary, add more water (keep the water at the level of the beans). Uncover the pot for the last 30 minutes of cooking to brown the beans. Serve with the prepared *Red Lion Inn Applesauce* and brown bread.

SERVES 6

Red Lion Inn Applesauce

10 large McIntosh apples, unpeeled, cored, and quartered
¹/₄ cup packed light brown sugar
¹/₄ cup sugar
1 tablespoon ground cinnamon

1. Place the apple quarters in a large saucepan and add 1" water. Cover and bring to a boil. Reduce heat and simmer until tender and soft, about 40 minutes. Do not burn.

2. Add both sugars and the cinnamon. Cover and simmer until all of the sugar is dissolved, about 10 minutes.

3. Pass the apple mixture through a food mill fitted with a fine blade or process in a food processor. Serve warm or chilled.

SERVES 6

"But since he stood for England
And knows what England means,
Unless you give him bacon
You must not give him beans."

— Baked beans and bacon were a common dish in England, often served to workers by employers during the Christmas/New Years' holidays, which inspired G.K. Chesterton (referring to laborers) to pen this poem.

Red Lion Inn Beef Stew

$^1\!/_3$ *cup flour*
salt and black pepper
2 pounds beef stew meat, trimmed and cut into $^3\!/_4$"-1" cubes
vegetable oil
1 $^1\!/_4$ pounds onions, cut into 1 $^1\!/_2$" cubes (about 2 cups)
6 cups beef broth
1 $^1\!/_2$ cups diced canned tomatoes
1 tablespoon dried oregano
1 $^1\!/_2$ tablespoons dried basil
1 $^1\!/_2$ teaspoons garlic powder
1 teaspoon Worcestershire sauce
$^1\!/_2$ cup red burgundy wine
2 bay leaves
4 quarts water
1 teaspoon salt
1 pound potatoes, peeled and cut into 1 $^1\!/_2$" cubes (about 2 cups)
$^2\!/_3$ cup carrots, cut into $^1\!/_2$" cubes
1 $^1\!/_2$ cups celery, cut into $^1\!/_2$" cubes
$^1\!/_2$ cup tiny pearl onions
$^1\!/_2$ cup frozen peas
salt and black pepper to taste

1. Place the flour in a shallow dish and season with the salt and black pepper. Dredge the beef in the seasoned flour, shaking off any excess.

2. In a heavy Dutch oven, heat enough oil to cover the bottom by $^1\!/_4$". Add the beef and sauté over medium-high heat until well browned, about 10-12 minutes. Add the cubed onions and sauté until the onions are browned and very lightly caramelized, about 8-10 minutes.

3. Add the broth, stirring well with a wooden spoon, and scraping the bottom of the pan. Bring to a boil. Reduce heat and simmer for 35-40 minutes. Add the tomatoes, herbs, garlic powder, Worcestershire sauce, wine, and bay leaves and simmer gently for 30 minutes more.

4. Bring the water to a boil in another pot. Add the salt, potatoes, and carrots and cook for 3 minutes, then add the celery and pearl onions and cook until the vegetables are just tender, about 7-9 minutes more. Add the peas and cook for 2 minutes more.

5. Drain the vegetables and add to the beef stew. Simmer the stew for 5 minutes. Remove the bay leaves and adjust the seasonings. Serve hot.

SERVES 10-12

"Long ago, at the end of the route,
The stage pulled up, and the folks stepped out.
They have all passed under the tavern door —
The youth and his bride and the gray three-score.
Their eyes were weary with dust and gleam,
The day had gone like an empty dream.
Soft may they slumber, and trouble no more
For their eager journey, its jolt and roar,
Has come to an end at the inn's door."

— Old Tavern Song

Chicken-Mushroom Pot Pie

¹/₂ cup butter
¹/₂ cup flour
3 cups chicken stock
3 cups veal stock
4 tablespoons olive oil
1 cup coarsely chopped onions
¹/₄ cup minced garlic
2 tablespoons chopped fresh rosemary
1 pound chorizo sausage, sliced into ¹/₂" pieces
2 cups coarsely chopped fresh mushrooms
2 cooked chicken breasts, diced
salt and black pepper to taste
1 package puff pastry shells, prepared

1. Melt the butter in a saucepan, then add the flour, stirring together until bubbly and very lightly browned, creating a roux. Slowly add 1 cup of the chicken stock, stirring constantly, until the mixture has thickened. Add another cup of the chicken stock and stir again until all of the ingredients are blended and the stock has thickened. Add the remaining chicken stock and veal stock and heat until the velouté has thickened slightly. Do not brown. Set aside.

2. Heat 2 tablespoons of the oil in a large sauté pan and sauté the onions, garlic, and rosemary over medium heat until soft and translucent, about 3-5 minutes. Add the sausage. Remove the mixture from the pan and set aside.

3. Heat the remaining oil in the same pan and sauté the mushrooms until the mushroom liquid has evaporated and the mushrooms are lightly browned. Add the reserved onion mixture and mix together well.

4. Add the diced chicken, the reserved velouté sauce, the salt, and black pepper to the mushroom mixture and mix together. Spoon the combined mixture into the prepared puff pastry shells and top with a puff pastry wheel. Serve immediately.

SERVES 6

Creamed Chicken Red Lion in Pastry Shells

4 whole chicken breasts, boned and skinned
2 cups chicken broth
1 package puff pastry shells
2 tablespoons dry sherry
2 tablespoons sauterne wine
³/₄ cup diced red bell peppers
³/₄ cup diced green bell peppers
¹/₂ cup sliced fresh mushrooms
¹/₂ cup frozen peas
2 cups Cream Sauce (see recipe below)
salt and white pepper to taste
2 tablespoons chopped fresh parsley, for garnish

   1. Combine the chicken breasts and broth in a large pot and bring to a boil over high heat. Skim off any foam that rises to the surface. Reduce heat and simmer until the chicken is tender, about 15-20 minutes. Remove the chicken from the pot and allow to cool. Cut the chicken into medium-sized cubes.

   2. Meanwhile, prepare and bake the pastry shells according to package directions. When golden brown and baked, remove the shells from the oven, then remove the tops, setting aside to use later. Scoop out the doughy insides and discard. Return the hollowed-out shells to the oven for 2 minutes, just long enough to dry out the insides.

   3. Combine the sherry and sauterne in a skillet over medium heat. Add both bell peppers and the mushrooms and sauté until just start to soften, about 4-5 minutes. Add the peas and chicken cubes and heat through. Add the prepared *Cream Sauce* and heat through but do not boil. Add the salt and white pepper.

   4. Spoon the creamed chicken into the prepared pastry shells and place the tops back in place. Garnish with the parsley and serve.

SERVES 6

Cream Sauce

¹/₄ cup butter
¹/₄ cup flour

2 cups light cream
2 small onions studded with 3 cloves
2 bay leaves
salt and black pepper to taste
ground nutmeg to taste

1. Melt the butter in a saucepan. Stir in the flour and cook over low heat for 3-4 minutes to form a roux. Do not brown.

2. In another saucepan, bring the cream just to a boil. Stir the warm cream into the flour mixture, whipping until smooth.

3. Add the onions and bay leaves and simmer over low heat for 20 minutes. Season with the salt, black pepper, and nutmeg. Strain the sauce and serve.

YIELD 2 CUPS

Jacks Salmon Cakes

Jack's restaurant is a casual spot in an atmospheric old building with wooden floors in the village of Housatonic — a mill town where several paper mills once operated. There's still one paper mill, but one of the massive brick buildings now houses the Housatonic Curtain Company, where many of the products for Country Curtains are manufactured. Jacks Grill is named for Jack Fitzpatrick. Its logo features a treasured old truck that he loves to drive.

1 pound fresh salmon fillet
salt and black pepper
1 medium onion, finely chopped
2 stalks celery, finely chopped
1 tablespoon Old Bay seasoning
³/₄ cup mayonnaise
¹/₄ cup fresh lemon juice
1 ¹/₂ cups Japanese bread crumbs (panko), or fresh bread crumbs
2 tablespoons olive oil
Rémoulade (see recipe on page 186)

1. Preheat oven to 350° F. Grease a baking pan large enough for the fillet to lie flat.

2. Sprinkle the fillet with the salt and black pepper and place in the prepared pan. Roast the fillet until cooked through, about 8-10 minutes. Allow to cool, then flake with a fork.

3. Combine the onion, celery, Old Bay seasoning, mayonnaise, and lemon juice in a bowl. Add the cooled salmon and gently mix together.

4. Add 1 cup of the bread crumbs and mix together lightly with hands, forming cakes of 5-6 tablespoons each. Do not overmix. Consistency should be light and fluffy.

5. Heat the oil in a sauté pan and dredge each salmon cake in the remaining bread crumbs and pan sear until golden brown. Turn each cake over and brown the other side. Keep hot in the oven until ready to serve. Serve with the prepared *Rémoulade.*

SERVES 2

Crab & Cod Cakes with Rémoulade & Corn Relish

$^1/_2$ pound salt cod
4 cups milk
$^1/_2$ pound fresh cod
$^1/_2$ pound crabmeat
1 cup mashed potatoes
$^1/_2$ bunch fresh chives, rinsed and chopped
$^3/_4$ cup mayonnaise
2 cups Japanese bread crumbs (panko), or fresh bread crumbs
$^1/_4$ cup Dijon mustard
salt and black pepper to taste
Old Bay seasoning to taste
flour for dredging
2 eggs, beaten
2 tablespoons corn oil
Rémoulade (see recipe below)
Corn Relish (see recipe below)

1. Combine the salt cod and 2 cups of the milk in a saucepan. Cover and refrigerate overnight or for at least 8 hours until the salt cod is soft. Place the soft cod in milk over low heat and poach gently until cooked through.

2. Heat the remaining milk in another saucepan, then add the fresh cod. Poach gently over low heat until cooked.

3. Flake the crabmeat and both cooked cods into a bowl. Add the potatoes and chives and mix together well.

4. Combine the mayonnaise, 1 cup of the bread crumbs, and the mustard in a bowl. Lightly toss with the crabmeat/cod mixture. Do not overmix (consistency should be light and fluffy). Add the salt, black pepper, and Old Bay seasoning.

5. Form the mixture into flat cakes or cylinders. Dredge each in the flour, then dip in the eggs, and then roll in the remaining bread crumbs. Cover and chill in the refrigerator until ready to serve.

6. Heat the oil in a skillet and fry the cakes over medium heat until golden brown and crisp on the outside.

7. Place on individual plates and spoon the prepared *Rémoulade* on the plate, with the prepared *Corn Relish* on the side. Serve hot.

SERVES 5-6

Rémoulade

¹/₄ cup drained capers
2 tablespoons minced shallots
¹/₄ cup whole grain mustard
1 clove garlic, minced
1 tablespoon minced gherkins
1 ¹/₂ teaspoons minced anchovies
2 cups mayonnaise

2 tablespoons minced fresh chives
2 tablespoons minced fresh tarragon
2 tablespoons whole black mustard seeds
2 tablespoons whole yellow mustard seeds
fresh lemon juice to taste
Worchestershire sauce to taste

1. Combine the capers, shallots, mustard, garlic, gherkins, and anchovies in a food processor and pulse gently until blended.

2. Place the processed mixture in a bowl and add the mayonnaise, herbs, and spices and mix together well. Season with the lemon juice and Worcestershire sauce. Chill in the refrigerator for at least 1 hour or until ready to use.

YIELD 2¹/₂ CUPS

Corn Relish

1 small white onion
¹/₂ cup roasted red peppers
2 cups fresh-cut corn
¹/₄ cup sugar
2 cups red wine vinegar
2 cups balsamic vinegar

1. Combine the onion and peppers in a food processor and pulse gently until ground, but chunky.

2. Mix together the processed mixture and the corn in a saucepan. Add the sugar and both vinegars and simmer gently until the corn is tender and the vinegars have evaporated, about 15 minutes.

3. Place the relish in a covered container and refrigerate until ready to use.

YIELD 2¹/₂ CUPS

Seafood Crêpes

¹/₂ pound fresh scallops, diced
¹/₂ pound small fresh shrimp, cleaned, peeled, and deveined
¹/₂ pound fresh haddock, cod, sole, or any firm white fish, diced
2 cups Cream Sauce (see recipe on pages 182-183)
¹/₄ cup sherry
salt and black pepper to taste
1 teaspoon ground paprika
10-12 Crêpes (see recipe below)
Seafood Newburg Sauce (see recipe below)

1. Preheat oven to 325° F. Grease a 7" x 11" baking dish.

2. Place the scallops, shrimp, and fish in a large steamer over simmering water. Steam the seafood until tender, about 10 minutes.

3. To the prepared *Cream Sauce,* add the sherry, then stir in the salt, black pepper, and paprika. Add the seafood and cook for 1-2 minutes to coat with the sauce.

4. Place approximately ¹/₈ cup of the seafood and sauce in the center of each prepared crêpe and roll up, encasing the filling. Place the crêpes side by side in the prepared dish. Pour ¹/₂ cup of the prepared *Seafood Newburg Sauce* over the crêpes and bake until hot and bubbly, about 8-10 minutes.

5. Serve 2 crêpes per person, with additional sauce on the side.

SERVES 5-6

Crêpes

2 eggs, at room temperature
1 ¹/₄ cups milk, at room temperature
1 cup flour
¹/₄ teaspoon salt
¹/₄ teaspoon clarified butter (see page 44)

1. Whip the eggs in a stainless bowl until thoroughly beaten.

2. Add the milk, flour, salt, and butter, and whip until smooth. Let stand, covered, for 1 hour to release air bubbles.

3. Lightly oil a crêpe pan or small omelette pan and heat over medium heat. Drop $\frac{1}{8}$ cup of the batter into the pan and quickly tilt the pan to evenly coat the bottom. The batter should be thin and even, with no holes or gaps. Cook gently until lightly browned on the edges, about 1-2 minutes. Turn the crêpe over and cook for 1 minute more.

4. As the crêpes are cooked, stack on a platter and keep warm in the oven. The crêpes can be made a day ahead and wrapped tighly in plastic wrap. Warm slightly when ready to use.

YIELD 18-22 CRÊPES

Seafood Newburg Sauce

2 tablespoons butter
2 teaspoons minced shallots
2 tablespoons ground paprika
$\frac{1}{2}$ cup dry sherry
2 tablespoons tomato paste
2 tablespoons brandy
2 cups Cream Sauce (see recipe on pages 182-183)
pinch dried thyme
pinch cayenne pepper

1. Melt the butter in a sauté pan. Add the shallots and sauté over medium heat until the shallots are translucent, about 2-3 minutes. Stir in the paprika and sherry and sauté for 2 minutes. Mix in the tomato paste.

2. Add the brandy and carefully light with a match. When the alcohol has burned off, add the prepared *Cream Sauce,* thyme, and cayenne pepper and cook for 2 minutes more.

YIELD 2 $\frac{1}{2}$ CUPS

Welsh Rarebit

2 cups milk
1 bay leaf
³/₄ cup butter
¹/₄ cup flour
¹/₈ teaspoon ground nutmeg
2 cups grated sharp cheddar cheese
¹/₂ cup beer
¹/₂ cup chicken broth
1 teaspoon ground paprika

¹/₂ teaspoon tomato paste
1 teaspoon Worcestershire sauce
¹/₈ teaspoon prepared English mustard
salt to taste
10 slices Canadian bacon
10 thick tomato slices
5 English muffins, split
ground paprika
chopped fresh parsley, for garnish

1. Heat the milk with the bay leaf in a small saucepan.

2. Melt ¹/₄ cup of the butter in another saucepan. Stir in the flour and cook for 2-3 minutes to form a roux. Do not brown. Remove the bay leaf and whisk the hot milk into the roux and cook, stirring constantly, until thick and creamy, about 6-8 minutes. Stir in the nutmeg.

3. Add the cheese, beer, broth, 1 teaspoon paprika, tomato paste, Worcestershire sauce, mustard, and salt to the roux. Mix thoroughly and cook slowly over low heat until the cheese is melted, about 5 minutes. Adjust the seasonings. Remove the saucepan from the heat, cover, and keep warm until ready to use.

4. Grill the bacon and tomato slices on a grill or under the broiler until lightly browned. Toast the muffins and spread the muffins with the remaining butter. Top each muffin with a slice of the grilled bacon and grilled tomato slice.

5. Pour ¹/₂ cup of the sauce over each rarebit. Sprinkle with the paprika and place under the broiler until lightly browned and bubbly, about 2 minutes. Garnish with the parsley and serve immediately.

SERVES 5

According to the New England Cookbook, *Welsh Rarebit (or Rabbit, as it is sometimes called by older New England cooks) should be "made from a Cheddar made in June from cow's milk that has in it the sweetness of New England buttercups. . . . It is not true that a Welsh Rabbit will keep you awake!" Ale or beer was almost always a necessary ingredient, and The Red Lion Inn's version holds true to traditional form.*

Corn Fritters

When the sugarhouses in northern Berkshire County start their production of maple syrup in early March, many of them open makeshift breakfast halls, where they serve pancakes and corn fritters with fresh maple syrup, direct from the vat. Is there anything sweeter? Outside the sugarshacks, the line in the snappy cold is often several country blocks long. Inside, the chairs are made from sawn logs, and the tables, set family-style, are made from huge slabs of maple. At The Red Lion Inn, you can dine on the same corn fritters with fresh maple syrup and *Red Lion Inn Breakfast Sausage* (see recipe on page 200) in a more refined atmosphere — and they're every bit as good.

1 ¹/₂ cups canned whole kernel corn
1 ¹/₂ cups canned creamed corn
5 eggs, separated
¹/₄ teaspoon salt
¹/₃ cup milk
1 ¹/₂ cups flour
1 tablespoon baking powder
¹/₃ cup sugar
confectioners' sugar
pure maple syrup, for serving

1. Heat a deep fryer filled with vegetable oil to 325° F.

2. Combine both corns in a bowl. Add the egg yolks to the corn and mix well.

3. In another bowl, beat the egg whites to form soft peaks. Add the salt and continue to beat until the egg whites form stiff peaks.

4. Add the milk to the corn mixture, then add the flour, baking powder, and sugar and mix together well. Fold in the stiff egg whites.

5. Using a small ice-cream scoop, drop scoops of dough into the hot fat and fry until golden brown and cooked completely. Remove the fritters from the fat and drain on paper towels. Dust with the confectioners' sugar. Serve the fritters with the maple syrup.

SERVES 8-10

CHAPTER 15

A Red Lion Inn Breakfast

When Calvin Coolidge, a native of Massachusetts and a frequent visitor to The Red Lion Inn, was in the White House, he insisted on continuing his New England breakfasts, which consisted of a hot cereal made from unground wheat and rye and corn muffins made according to an old New England recipe. Traditional New England corn muffins are often available today at The Red Lion Inn, as they have been for many years.

James Beard in *American Cookery* remarked: "I'm sure we lead the world, as we always have, on the subject of breakfast eggs. Our variety of egg and meat combinations for this meal is unequaled when we begin to tally ham and eggs, and sausage, meat or link, and eggs. And we are the only country I can think of where potatoes are important as a breakfast food — hashed brown or country-fried or cottage-fried potatoes — combined with eggs, or meat and eggs."

One of the most enduringly popular breakfast treats at The Red Lion Inn, however, is old-fashioned oatmeal, served steaming hot with brown sugar and raisins. Popular variations offer oatmeal served with chopped dates and maple syrup, with bananas and honey, or with dried apples added just before serving. The popularity of oatmeal probably stems from the fact that The Red Lion Inn is one of the few restaurants remaining that serves oatmeal at all. It's a lasting reminder of the timelessness of The Red Lion Inn.

"Yet, who can help loving the land that has taught us Six hundred and eighty-five ways to dress eggs?"

— Thomas Moore, *The Fudge Family in Paris,* 1818

Eggs Benedict with Canadian Bacon

This recipe may be varied by substituting smoked salmon slices for the Canadian bacon, a dill hollandaise sauce for the regular hollandaise, salmon roe for the black olives, and a dill sprig for the parsley.

2 English muffins, split
¹/₄ cup butter
2 quarts water
4 eggs
4 slices Canadian bacon
Hollandaise Sauce (see recipe on page 83-84)
4 black olives, sliced, for garnish
¹/₄ cup chopped fresh parsley, for garnish

1. Toast the English muffins and spread with the butter. Keep warm and crisp in a warm oven.

2. Bring the water to a slow simmer in a shallow saucepan. Crack the eggs, one at a time, into a cup or saucer, then slide the eggs into the poaching water. Poach until cooked to taste, about 5-8 minutes.

3. Meanwhile, grill the bacon slices and place one on each English muffin half. Remove the eggs from the poaching water with a slotted spoon and drain. If desired, trim the edges with kitchen shears or a knife to remove irregular edges. Place 1 poached egg on top of each muffin half and spoon the prepared *Hollandaise Sauce* on top. Garnish with the olives and parsley. Serve immediately.

SERVES 2

Frittata

8 eggs
4 cups heavy cream
1 tablespoon olive oil
$^1/_2$ medium white onion, julienned
$^1/_4$ cup quartered fresh crimini mushrooms
$^1/_4$ cup quartered fresh shiitake mushrooms
$^1/_4$ cup trimmed fresh oyster mushrooms
4 sprigs fresh thyme, rinsed and chopped
salt and black pepper to taste

1. Preheat oven to 325° F.

2. Whisk the eggs in a bowl until frothy. Add the cream and whisk together well.

3. Heat the oil in a large, ovenproof sauté pan. Add the onion and sauté until slightly caramelized. Add all of the mushrooms, the thyme, salt, and black pepper and sauté until the mushroom liquid is evaporated.

4. Stir in the egg mixture. Remove the pan from the stove and bake in the oven until the frittata is slightly browned and puffed.

5. Cut the frittata into 6 wedges and place on individual plates. Serve immediately.

SERVES 6

Salmon Omelette with Sour Cream, Dill & Salmon Caviar

12 eggs
$^1/_2$ cup clarified butter (see page 44)
12 slices smoked salmon
$^1/_2$ cup sour cream
2 tablespoons plus 2 teaspoons chopped fresh dill
4 teaspoons salmon caviar
4 sprigs fresh dill

1. Whisk the eggs in a stainless steel or glass bowl until foamy.

2. Melt 2 tablespoons of the butter in an omelette pan over medium heat. Pour one-fourth of the beaten eggs into the pan. As the eggs begin to set, roll the pan from side to side, covering the bottom. When set on the bottom, flip the omelette over. Lay 3 slices of the smoked salmon, 1 tablespoon of the sour cream, and 1 teaspoon of the chopped dill on top.

3. When the omelette is set on the second side, roll or fold in half. Remove from heat and place on a warm plate. Slit the top of the omelette and spoon 1 tablespoon more of the sour cream into the slit. Sprinkle the caviar over the sour cream and top with 1 dill sprig.

4. Repeat three times, with the remaining ingredients. Serve immediately.

SERVES 4

Berkshire Apple Pancake

This popular Red Lion Inn recipe uses two products from the bounty of the Berkshires — apples and pure maple syrup.

3 apples, peeled and cored
3 eggs, beaten
3 cups flour
1 ¹/₂ tablespoons baking powder
³/₄ teaspoon salt
5 tablespoons sugar
2 cups milk
³/₄ teaspoon vanilla
³/₄ teaspoon ground cinnamon
5 tablespoons butter
¹/₄ cup firmly packed light brown sugar
warm, pure maple syrup, for serving

1. Preheat oven to 450° F.

2. Coarsely chop 2¹/₂ of the apples. Slice the remaining ¹/₂ apple into thin spirals for garnish on top. Brush the spirals with lemon juice to prevent them from darkening and set aside.

3. Mix together the eggs, flour, baking powder, salt, sugar, milk, vanilla, cinnamon, and the chopped apples in a bowl. Stir until well combined, although the batter will remain lumpy.

4. Melt the butter in a 10" cast-iron skillet. Pour the batter into the skillet and arrange the reserved apple spirals on top.

5. Bake the pancake for 15 minutes. Reduce temperature to 350° and continue to bake for 40 minutes more, or until a toothpick inserted in the center comes out clean. Remove the skillet from the oven and let stand for 5 minutes.

6. Sprinkle the brown sugar over the top of the pancake, cut into wedges, and serve with the maple syrup.

SERVES 6

Buttermilk Pancakes with Blueberries

At The Red Lion Inn, breakfast pancakes are often served with berries or fruits in season. That might mean strawberries, blueberries, apples, or even bananas.

1 pint fresh blueberries (or other fruit in season)
7 eggs
2 cups buttermilk
2 ¹/₂ cups flour
1 ¹/₂ teaspoons baking soda
1 ¹/₂ teaspoons salt
4 ¹/₂ teaspoons baking powder
1 tablespoon vegetable shortening, melted
warm, pure maple syrup, for serving

1. Preheat a griddle to medium heat. Lightly oil the griddle.
2. Rinse the blueberries and discard stems, shrunken berries, and impurities.
3. Whip together the eggs and buttermilk in a large bowl.
4. Combine all of the dry ingredients in a separate bowl, then add to the buttermilk mixture. Add the melted shortening and mix well. Do not overmix. Keep the mixture somewhat lumpy.
5. Using a ¹/₄ cup ladle, pour the batter onto the prepared griddle. Sprinkle 1 tablespoon of the blueberries on top of each pancake. Cook until bubbles appear on top, about 3-4 minutes. Turn over and cook for 2-3 minutes on the other side. Serve immediately with the maple syrup.

SERVES 6-8

> *"I said my prayers and ate some cranberry tart for breakfast."*
>
> — From the dairy of William Byrd, 1711

French Toast Royale

1 cup milk
³/₄ teaspoon ground cinnamon
³/₈ teaspoon ground nutmeg
1 tablespoon fresh orange juice
³/₄ teaspoon vanilla
5 eggs
8-10 slices Challah (see recipe on page 76)
confectioners' sugar
pure maple syrup

1. Mix together the milk, cinnamon, nutmeg, and orange juice in a saucepan and heat over low heat until barely simmers. Remove from heat and allow to cool. Add the vanilla.

2. Beat together the eggs and the cooled milk mixture in a large shallow bowl.

3. Dip each slice of the prepared *Challah* in the egg mixture, covering both sides. In a lightly buttered skillet over low-medium heat, sauté the bread until golden brown, about 4-5 minutes on each side.

4. Sprinkle the confectioners' sugar over the bread and serve 2-3 slices per person with the maple syrup on the side.

SERVES 4

Red Lion Inn Roast Beef Hash

1 ¹/₄ pounds cooked prime rib or roast beef, trimmed of fat and gristle
³/₄ pound potatoes, peeled, cooked, and diced
¹/₂ pound onions, quartered
¹/₂ teaspoon salt
¹/₂ teaspoon black pepper
1 teaspoon dried thyme
1 teaspoon garlic powder
¹/₂ teaspoon dried marjoram
1 tablespoon Worcestershire sauce
¹/₄ cup vegetable oil
12 eggs

1. Cut the beef into 1" cubes.

2. Combine the beef cubes, potatoes, onions, and seasonings in a large bowl and mix thoroughly. Set aside, covered, for 2 hours.

3. Coarsely dice or chop the meat mixture with a meat grinder or food processor, but do not allow to get mushy.

4. Heat the oil in a heavy skillet and cook the hash over medium heat until the potatoes are brown. Turn the hash over and cook the other side. Adjust the seasonings.

5. While the hash is cooking, fry or poach the eggs. Top each portion of hash with 2 eggs and serve immediately.

SERVES 6

Mrs. Harriet Martineau, author of Society in America *(1837) and* Retrospect of Western Travel *(1838) stayed in Stockbridge, probably at The Red Lion Inn, and noted that she breakfasted on "excellent bread, potatoes, hung beef, eggs, and strong tea at Stockbridge, Mass."*

Red Lion Inn Home Fries

2 pounds potatoes, peeled and cut into $^1/_4$" cubes
1 cup butter
$^3/_4$ cup diced onions
2 tablespoons Home Fries Seasoning Mix (see recipe below)
butter, for serving (optional)

1. Cook the potatoes in a vegetable steamer over simmering water until just tender, about 20-30 minutes.

2. Melt the 1 cup butter in a heavy skillet. Add the onions and 1 tablespoon of the prepared *Home Fries Seasoning Mix* and sauté over medium heat until the onions are limp and translucent, about 10 minutes. Do not brown.

3. Add the steamed potatoes, sprinkle with the remaining seasoning mix, and sauté over medium heat until golden brown and crisp, about 15 minutes. If desired, dot with the butter for added flavor. Serve.

SERVES 8

Home Fries Seasoning Mix

This seasoning mix is used for a variety of dishes. Sprinkle over roasted potatoes or rub into the skin of a chicken before roasting.

1 cup salt
$^1/_2$ cup ground paprika
$^1/_4$ cup black pepper
$^1/_4$ cup white pepper
$^1/_2$ cup onion powder
$^1/_2$ cup garlic salt

Combine all of the ingredients in a large jar or other covered container and shake to mix well. The mix will last up to 6 months.

YIELD 3 CUPS

Red Lion Inn Breakfast Sausage

If you won't be cooking this sausage within 24 hours of preparation, store in the freezer. It will keep frozen for up to 3 months.

6 pounds boneless pork butt, trimmed of sinew and gristle
$^1/_4$ cup salt
$^1/_4$ cup ground sage
1 $^1/_2$ tablespoons cayenne pepper
1 $^1/_2$ tablespoons light brown sugar

1. Cut the pork with its fat into 1" cubes.
2. Mix together the seasonings and brown sugar in a large bowl. Add the pork cubes and toss well. Cover and chill overnight.
3. Grind the sausage once (for a coarse, country-style sausage) in a well-chilled meat grinder with a $^1/_8$" blade. Shape into patties or roll the sausage up in parchment paper to form a cylinder and slice $^1/_2$" thick. Pan grill or broil, as desired.

YIELD 6 POUNDS

"The critical period in matrimony is breakfast-time."

— A.P. Herbert

Old-Fashioned Oatmeal

Popular Red Lion Inn variations include oatmeal served with chopped dates and maple syrup, with bananas and honey, or with dried apples.

2 cups rolled oats (stone ground, if available)
3 cups cold water
1 cup cold milk
$^1/_4$ teaspoon salt
2 tablespoons light brown sugar
1 tablespoon raisins

1. Combine the oats, water, milk, and salt in a large saucepan and bring to a boil. Cook slowly for 5 minutes. Remove from heat and let stand until desired consistency (it will thicken as it stands).

2. Sprinkle the oatmeal with the brown sugar and raisins and serve immediately.

SERVES 6

CHAPTER 16

Cocktails & Drinks

In the early days, a tavern's prosperity depended chiefly on the warmth of its log fire and the fire in its punch. The following description from *Stage-Coach and Tavern Days* demonstrates the importance of tavern libations: "A man can never make good punch unless he is satisfied, nay positive, that no man breathing can make better. I retire to a solitary corner with my ingredients ready sorted; they are as follows, and I mix them in the order they are here written. Sugar, twelve tolerable lumps; hot water, one pint; lemons, two, the juice and peel; old Jamaica rum, two gills; brandy, one gill; porter or stout, half a gill; arrack, a slight dash. I allow myself five minutes to make a bowl in the foregoing proportions, carefully stirring the mixture as I furnish the ingredients until it actually foams; and then Kangaroos! How beautiful it is!"

Flips were warm winter drinks that were heated by thrusting an iron flip dog (fire poker) into the mug, which produced a sizzle and a burnt taste. According to the editors of *The American Heritage Cookbook*, a frequent early traveler, Myles Arnold, insisted that the flip was especially popular with the riders on the Boston Post route: "and indeed, 'tis said they sometimes wrap themselves warmly with it."

When Silas Pepoon owned The Red Lion Inn, tavern parties were festive affairs. Accounts claim that there were dancing and merrymaking among the young people. The ladies sipped wine and cider and a headier drink, the flip, while the gentlemen indulged in even more fiery and exciting beverages. When parties were not going on, Pepoon handed out hot punches and rum toddies over the bar in the public room and lamented the horrible condition of the roads (the west end of Main Street had a way of disappearing under water when the Housatonic River flooded the meadows).

According to Eleanor Early in her *New England Cookbook*, cider was a staple of the

When The Red Lion Inn sought a liquor
license in 1934 after ninety-five dry years, a
sometime local resident penned this poem:

Yes, ninety-five long years have passed
Since first mine host, Pepoon,
Regarding well his pots and pans
And platters, knives, and spoon.

While Bingham, Kingsley, and John Hicks
In order passed along;
And at the corner of the Inn
A haughty lion hung.

Red was his color, and his name,
He braved the summer's heat
The winter's cold, with ice and snow
That never chilled his feet.
Then Kingsley, Rockwell, Gilpin, Plumb,
Pilling and Heaton, too —
What hosts they were, as fine a lot
As e're one ever knew.

And not a dram of liquor served,
No, not one tiny drop.
A thirst that must be satisfied
Must seek another shop.

Red Lion Inn was dry forsooth
In rafter and in mood,
And in the wee small hours of night
Would crack and creak and brood; —

O'er juleps, punches, stirrup cups,
And ale, upon the draught,
With spirits in that hostelry
To promulgate its craft.
And thoughts symbolic of its sign
So bold, (just stop and think),

A Lion, and e'en Red at that,
And not a drop to drink.

But times have changed since old Pepoon
In his good ways was set,
For in the race to hold the pace
The Inn is going "wet,"

Ye shades of Bingham, Plumb, and Hicks,
Kingsley, and Heaton too,
What kind of punch, of widespread fame,
Will the "Red Lion" brew?

— Edward P. Merwin

early tavern bar. New Englanders had been making hard cider since well before the Revolution, as a way to use up some of the apples that their trees produced. Even today, a crock of steaming cider is ready for guests in The Lion's Den, the downstairs "pub" at The Red Lion Inn.

Cheap molasses from the West Indies created the highly profitable New England rum industry, which played such an important role in early trade. According to historian Samuel Eliot Morison: "The West Indies trade was the main factor in New England prosperity until the American Revolution; without it, the settlements on the northern coast would have remained stationary or declined." Once they began importing molasses, rum or "Kill Devil" became the drink of preference in taverns.

All drinks were not consumed in taverns, however. It was often the chore of housewives to brew a variety of homemade drinks to have on hand for visitors. Root and de

Rochemont in *Eating in America* say: "The early nineteenth-century housewife brewed the family drinks — beers (ginger, spruce, sassafras, molasses); wines (elderberry, elder flower, gooseberry, currant, raspberry, and cider wine); cordials (cherry, strawberry, lemon, rose, aniseed); brandies (rose, lemon); punches (Roman, milk, Regent's) — and fox grape shrub, cherry bounce, ratafia, capillaire, orgeat, bishop, egg nogg [sic], sangaree, negus, Turkish sherbet, and, God help us, sassafras mead."

By the twentieth century, The Red Lion Inn was apparently in the forefront of Prohibition and an unwilling participant in its repeal. The *Berkshire Evening Eagle* on July 19, 1934, reported that no drinking had taken place in The Red Lion Inn for almost 100 years, and even though Prohibition was repealed in 1933, Congressman Allen T. Treadway's establishment was, a year later, still a most reluctant accessory in the "post-Prohibition hysteria." The article relates the tale of a couple who desired a cocktail before attending a play at the Stockbridge Playhouse. There was no bar at the inn, so they first asked the doorman and then the desk clerk where they might get a drink. After whispered conversations behind closed doors and an interminable wait, the couple was ushered into a private room where some ice, several glasses, a bottle of soda, and two portions of whiskey were laid out. "I suppose you'll pour your own," said the attendant, who quickly and silently left the room, closing the door behind him and leaving the couple to their own devises.

The word "cocktail" is probably not of New England origin, and there are several theories about its genesis. One is that a Frenchman, a Monsieur A.A. Peychaud, opened an apothecary shop in New Orleans in 1793 where he sometimes dispensed a concoction made of cognac and bitters to customers suffering from an unknown malady. He served the potion in a *coquetier,* or a French eggcup, which Americans could not pronounce properly and garbled into the word "cocktail." Another version says that he stirred the drink with a tail feather from a rooster.

Today, a variety of mixed drinks and wines are served in the Widow Bingham's Tavern and in The Lion's Den, as well as in the lobby or on the porch. Rum drinks are still popular at The Red Lion Inn, including a smooth, hot buttered rum and a holiday eggnog. The hot spiced cider is the perfect warmer-upper after a day on the nearby ski slopes.

Note: See Chapter 13, Holiday Time at The Red Lion Inn, for the recipes *Holiday Eggnog* and *Red Lion Inn Christmas Drink Glŏog.*

Bloody Mary

A tomato and vodka drink was invented at Harry's New York Bar in Paris by Fernand Petiot in the early 1920s. In 1934, Petiot became the bartender at New York's King Cole Bar in the St. Regis Hotel. One day when man-about-town Serge Obolensky requested his favorite drink, Petiot spiced it up with lemon, Worcestershire sauce, salt, and black pepper and created this new version. It was originally called the Bloody Mary after a Chicago club called The Bucket of Blood, but that name was deemed much too low class for such a high-class establishment. The name was therefore changed to the Red Snapper, but over the years, with the drink's enduring popularity, the original name gradually crept back in.

The Bloody Marys at The Red Lion Inn have been justifiably renowned for years. They are made with fresh ingredients, and each is individually prepared — no mixes used here!

1 ounce vodka
$^3/_4$ cup tomato juice
2 dashes fresh lemon juice
4 dashes Worcestershire sauce
2-3 drops Tabasco sauce
2 dashes salt
2 dashes black pepper
$^1/_4$ teaspoon prepared horseradish (optional)
fresh celery stalk, for garnish
lime wedge, for garnish

Combine the first eight ingredients in a hurricane glass and stir well. Garnish with the celery stalk and lime wedge. Serve.

SERVES 1

Piña Colada

This drink is one of the all-time favorites at The Red Lion Inn, especially when sipped in the summer courtyard, next to the lion statue.

1 ¹/₂ ounces light rum
6 tablespoons pineapple juice
4 tablespoons coconut cream
³/₄ cup ice
pineapple slice, for garnish

Place all of the ingredients, except the pineapple slice, into a blender. Blend at high speed for 15 seconds. Pour into a hurricane glass and garnish with the pineapple. Serve.

SERVES 1

Bingham's Blush

This delightful libation is named after the cozy Widow Bingham's Tavern at The Red Lion Inn.

1 ounce gin
6 tablespoons fresh orange juice
6 tablespoons fresh lemon juice
2 drops grenadine syrup
club soda, chilled

Shake the gin, both juices, and grenadine in a covered container with some shaved ice. Strain over ice into a collins glass and fill the glass with the club soda. Serve.

SERVES 1

Brandy Milk Punch

1 1/4 ounces brandy
3/4 cup chilled milk
1 teaspoon sugar
ground nutmeg

Shake the first three ingredients in a covered container with some shaved ice. Strain into a chilled collins glass and sprinkle with the nutmeg. Serve.

SERVES 1.

Hot Toddy

1 lump sugar
³/₄ cup boiling water
1 cinnamon stick, 1 ¹/₂" long
3 whole cloves
1 ¹/₄ ounces blended whiskey
lemon slice, for garnish

Dissolve the sugar in the boiling water in a heated mug. Add the cinnamon stick, cloves, and whiskey and stir. Garnish with the lemon slice and serve.

SERVES 1

Hot Buttered Rum

The editors of *The American Heritage Cookbook* provide us with the following information about hot buttered rum: "Nicholas Cresswell wrote in his journal in 1777 that the people of New England 'import large quantities of Molasses from the West Indies, which they distill and sell to Africa and the other Colonies, which goes by the name of Yankee Rum or Stink-e-buss.' Rum had become an important part of the American economy by the early seventeenth century, and the passage of the Molasses Act by the British Parliament in 1733 had done much to lay the foundation for the Revolution."

1 lump sugar
1 cinnamon stick, 1 $^1/_2$" long
2 whole cloves
$^3/_4$ cup boiling water
1 teaspoon butter
1 $^1/_4$ ounces dark rum
1 teaspoon pure maple syrup
ground nutmeg

Place the sugar, cinnamon stick, and cloves in a heated mug and add the boiling water. Add the butter, rum, and maple syrup and stir. Sprinkle with the nutmeg and serve.

SERVES 1

Benjamin Franklin's Orange Shrub

"*To a Gallon of Rum two Quarts of Orange Juice and two pound of Sugar — dissolve the Sugar in the Juice before you mix it with the Rum — put all together in a Cask & shake it well — let it stand 3 or 4 weeks and it will be very fine & fit for Bottling — when you have Bottled off the fine pass the thick thro' a Philtring paper put into a Funnell — that not a drop may be lost. To obtain the flavour of the Orange Peel paire a few Oranges & put it in Rum for twelve hours — & put that Rum into the Cask with the other — For Punch thought better without the Peel.*"

— American Philosophical Society, *The Franklin Papers*

Hot Spiced Cider

This drink is equally popular at The Red Lion Inn without the rum, as a hot, nonalcoholic drink.

1 ¹/₄ ounces dark rum
1 orange peel
1 cinnamon stick, 1 ¹/₂" long
2 whole cloves
6 ounces apple cider, heated
ground nutmeg

Pour all of the ingredients, except the nutmeg, into a heated mug. Let steep for 3 minutes, then stir. Sprinkle with the nutmeg and serve.

SERVES 1

Fitz Irish Coffee

1 ounce Kahlúa liqueur
1 ounce Irish whiskey
1 cup hot black coffee
fresh whipped cream
ground nutmeg

Place the liqueur into a heated mug or stemmed goblet. Add the whiskey and hot coffee and stir. Add a dollop of the whipped cream and sprinkle with the nutmeg. Serve.

SERVES 1.

Fitz Fizz

Children are an important part of the hospitality scene at The Red Lion Inn, so it's not surprising that special drinks have been created just for them. Standards, such as the Shirley Temple, are served at the inn, but so are *Fitz Fizz* and *Leo the Lion*.

2 tablespoons fresh lemon juice
2 tablespoons pineapple juice
2 tablespoons fresh orange juice
club soda
dash grenadine syrup
pineapple slice, for garnish

Shake all of the juices together in a covered container with some shaved ice. Pour the mixture over ice cubes in a collins glass. Top with the club soda. Add the grenadine and garnish with the pineapple. Serve.

SERVES 1

Leo the Lion

¹/₂ scoop raspberry sherbet
¹/₂ cup fresh orange juice
6 tablespoons club soda
1 orange slice, for garnish
1 maraschino cherry, for garnish

An early sign — now retired — for The Lion's Den.

DAVID MILTON JONES. COURTESY STOCKBRIDGE LIBRARY ASSOCIATION HISTORICAL ROOM

Place the sherbet and orange juice in a blender and blend at medium-high speed for 15 seconds. Pour into a glass and top with the club soda. Garnish with the orange slice and cherry. Serve.

SERVES 1

Pantry

INGREDIENTS

Some ingredients in the recipes in this cookbook are of a general nature and have not been specified in every recipe. The reader should note that the following ingredients have been assumed throughout the book, unless the recipe states otherwise.

butter: lightly salted butter
eggs: large
flour: all-purpose flour, sifted once before
        the measurement
milk: whole, pasteurized and homogenized
sugar: granulated sugar

DEFINITIONS

The following terms are used in many recipes in this cookbook:

Clarified butter: unsalted butter that has been allowed to melt slowly, allowing the milky solids to drift to the bottom of the pan and the clear liquid to rise to the top. It's this clear, top liquid that is known as clarified butter. Clarified butter does not burn as easily as whole butter and is preferred for sautéing delicate fish and chicken dishes and for bread rounds or croutons. Directions for making clarified butter are found on page 44.

Roux, a thickening agent for creamy sauces, is a combination of butter and flour slowly cooked together for several minutes before adding a liquid. Slow cooking eliminates the raw, pasty taste of uncooked flour and prepares the flour granules for absorption of the liquid. The procedure for making a roux is included in appropriate recipes.

Julienne: to slice into thin strips about the size of matchsticks.

Bibliography

American Heritage Magazine, the editors of *The American Heritage Cookbook.* New York: American Heritage Press, 1964.

America's Cook Book. Compiled by The Home Institute of *The New York Herald Tribune.* New York: Charles Scribner's Sons, 1938.

Anderson, Jean & Elaine Hanna. *The New Doubleday Cookbook.* Garden City, NY: Doubleday & Company, Inc., 1985.

"Anna Bingham: From The Red Lion to The Supreme Court," *The New England Quarterly,* Volume LXIX, Number 2, June 1996.

"Antique Hunters Comb Garrets of Farm Houses in Berkshire" *The Springfield Sunday Republican,* February 28, 1928.

Bass, Milton. "The Red Lion Inn." *The Berkshire Eagle,* July 29, 1973.

Beard, James. *American Cookery.* Boston: Little, Brown, and Company, 1972.

Beeton, Mrs. Isabella. *Beeton's Book of Household Management.* London: S.O. Beeton, 18 Bouverie St. E.C., 1861.

Begley, Sally. "Up Country." *The Berkshire Eagle,* December 3, 1973.

The Berkshire Eagle. 1934.

Berkshire Resort Topics. 1904.

Blake, Andrew. "Sweet Sculpture." *The Boston Sunday Globe,* March 26, 1978.

Brett, Jan. *The Gingerbread Baby.* New York: G. P. Putnam's Sons, 1999.

———. *The Night Before Christmas.* New York: G. P. Putnam's Sons, 1998.

Byrne, Robert. *1911 Best Things Anybody Ever Said.* New York: Fawcett Columbine, 1988.

Chadwick, Mrs. J. *Home Cookery.* Boston: 1853.

Chapman, Gerard. "Stockbridge Dog and Cat Fountain," *The Berkshire Eagle,* December 5, 1978.

———. *A History of The Red Lion Inn in Stockbridge, Massachusetts.* Stockbridge: The Red Lion Inn, 1987.

Child, Julia, et al. *Mastering the Art of French Cooking.* New York: Alfred A. Knopf, 1966.

Cobbett, William. *A Year's Residence in the United States of America.* 1819.

Day, Charles. *Hints on Etiquette.* 1844.

Doherty, Robert H., ed. *The First Ladies Cook Book.* New York: Parents Magazine Press, 1966.

Earle, Alice Morse. *Stage-Coach and Tavern Days.* New York: The Macmillan Company, 1900.

Early, Eleanor. *New England Cookbook.* New York: Random House, Inc., 1954.

Farmer, Fannie Merritt. *The Boston Cooking School Cook Book.* Boston: Little, Brown and Company, first published 1896, Sixth Ed., Completely Revised, 1940.

Field, Mrs. Stephen Johnson. *Statemen's Dishes and How to Cook Them.* 1890.

Forbes, Allan and Ralph M. Eastman. *Taverns and Stagecoaches of New England.* Boston: Printed by the State Street Trust Co., The Rand Press, 1954.

Franklin, Benjamin. "Homespun." *The Gazetteer,* January 2, 1766.

Harger, L.W. "First Red Lion Inn was Built in 1773." (name of newspaper unknown) Pittsfield, Massachusetts, June 7, 1912.

Lee, Hilde Gabriel. *Taste of the States: A Food History of America.* Charlottesville, VA: Howell Press, Inc., 1992.

Leonard, Jonathan Norton and the editors of Time-Life Books. *American Cooking: New England.* New York: Time-Life Books, 1970.

Leslie, Eliza. *Directions for Cookery.* Philadelphia, 1828 (Reprinted Arno Press, NY, 1973).

———. *Miss Leslie's Complete Cookery.* Philadelphia: E.L. Carey & A. Hart, 1837.

National Society of The Colonial Dames of America. *Old Inns of Connecticut.* Hartford, CT: The Prospect Press, 1937.

O'Connell, Jean. "Christmas Every Day at Gumdrop Square." *The Springfield Sunday Republican,* December 19, 1976.

Owens, Carole. *The Berkshire Cottages, A Vanishing Era.* Englewood Cliffs, NJ: Cottage Press, Inc., 1984.

Parker, James Reid. "Down From the Mountain." *The New Yorker,* September 4, 1948.

The People of Stockbridge, Massachusetts. *The Stockbridge Story 1739-1989.* Stockbridge, Massachusetts, 1989.

Price, Mary and Vincent. *A Treasury of Great Recipes.* U.S., Ampersand Press, Inc., 1965.

"Red Lion Inn Totally Destroyed by Fire This Morning." *The Pittsfield Evening Journal,* August 31, 1896.

Rombauer, Irma S. and Marion Rombauer Becker. *Joy of Cooking.* Indianapolis: The Bobbs-Merrill Company, Inc., 1964.

Root, Waverley. *Food.* New York: Konecky & Konecky, 1980.

———, and Richard de Rochemont. *Eating in America, A History.* New York: William Morrow and Company, Inc., 1976.

Sedgwick, Henry Dwight. *Memoirs of an Epicurean.* New York: The Bobbs-Merrill Company, 1942.

Sedgwick, Sarah Cabot and Christina Sedgwick Marquand. *Stockbridge 1739-1939, A Chronicle.* Great Barrington, MA: The Berkshire Courier, 1939.

"Sh-h-h Staid Old Red Lion Inn Sells a Drink of Liquor Amid Mysterious Motions." *Berkshire Evening Eagle,* 1934.

Simmons, Amelia. *American Cookery.* Reprint of the First Edition, New York, 1958.

The Springfield Union, September 12, 1943.

Stevens, William Oliver. *Discovering Long Island.* New York: Dodd, Mead & Company, 1939.

Stowe, Harriet Beecher. *Oldtown Folks, A Story of New England.* Reprint of 1869 edition, AMS Press, 1969.

Treadway, Heaton. *The Tale of the Lion.* Stockbridge, Massachusetts, The Red Lion Inn.

Tree, Christina. "A Passion for Inns." *The Boston Globe,* November 28, 1971.

Trollope, Frances. *Domestic Manners of the Americans.* Edited by Donald Smalley. New York: Alfred A. Knopf, 1949.

Willan, Anne. *Great Cooks and Their Recipes From Taillevent to Escoffier.* Boston: Little, Brown and Company, 1992.

The Women of General Foods Kitchens. *The General Foods Cookbook.* New York: Random House, 1959.

Index

About the Owners

The Fitzpatrick family have been the owners of The Red Lion Inn since 1968. Under their care it has grown in size and stature, and the restaurants are winning national acclaim. Shown in this picture: (center row) Jack and Jane Fitzpatrick; (back row) daughter Nancy, her husband, Lincoln Russell, and their son, Casey; (front row) daughter Ann and Ann's son, Alexander.

About the Author

Suzi Forbes Chase is a writer with an extensive culinary background. She has attended *Ecole de Cuisine La Varenne* in Paris, as well as *Peter Kump's Cooking School* in New York. She participated in a course taught by cookbook author Eileen Yin-Fei Lo at The China Institute in New York and she has also taken individual courses from Julia Child and Marchella and Victor Hazen. Her wine background includes a course at *l'Académie du Vin* in Paris, as well as numerous wine courses in the United States. She has been a restaurant reviewer and is currently the editor of *ZagatSurvey* to restaurants on Long Island. In addition, she has written eighteen travel books and is currently the author of three guidebooks to Country Inns and Bed and Breakfast establishments that she regularly updates, as well as *The Hamptons Book: A Complete Guide*. She is a member of the American Society of Journalists and Authors. She and her husband live on Long Island in New York State.